Chicken Soup to Warm the Neshama

101 Short Stories, Insights & Sayings
Containing Life-Long Lessons

Sixth Edition

Written & Compiled by
Pesach & Chana Burston

"This book brings readers the same lessons that charismatic speakers delivered to listeners in years past."

—The Jewish Week

"In everyone's life there are difficult moments, when one looks for a ray of light in the darkness. *Chicken Soup to Warm the Neshama* provides brief stories which can help a person smooth out the "bumps" in life."

—**Rabbi Dr. Abraham J. Twerski**
Founder and medical director of Gateway Rehabilitation Center, PA
International lecturer, author of more than sixty books and recipient of multiple awards

"Parables, anecdotes and aphorisms, like chicken-soup, come in varying flavors. They are all great remedies for greater insights, each with its own lesson, though not necessarily equally appealing to all. *Chicken Soup to Warm the Neshama* is a rich brew with invigorating offerings for all taste-buds to inspire personal growth and a desire to share them with others."

—**Rabbi Dr. J. Immanuel Schochet**
Noted author and lecturer. Rabbi of Congregation Beth Joseph
Professor-emeritus of Philosophy, Humber College, Toronto

"A book filled with sweetness, love, compassion and sensitivity, just like its two authors. Whoever is in need of any of these qualities would do well to read this book."

—**Rabbi Yosef Y. Jacobson**
Acclaimed international lecturer, Rabbi of Congregation Beis Shmuel of Crown Heights
Prolific writer of thousands of Torah essays and author of "A Tale of Two Souls"

"What's neat about these stories is the way we learn from them. We make a rational judgment on a real issue – in somebody else's life – and then start thinking, 'Hey, what about me in my own life?' This collection lets you laugh, cry, think hard, have fun and grow wiser all at once."

—**Rabbi Tzvi Freeman**
Author of numerous books including "Bringing Heaven Down to Earth"
as well as articles and essays on Jewish mysticism and practice

B"H.

Dedicated to
Our Children
Who are a constant reminder that
we should follow the lessons of the stories
as much as we like telling them

ॐ

© Copyright 2001, 2003, 2004, 2006, 2012, 2016
by Pesach & Chana Burston, Publishers

Sixth Edition 2016

Co-Distributed by
www.JewishInnovations.com
Info@JewishInnovations.com

Yossi Goodman Distributing
ChickenSoupNeshama@gmail.com

ISBN: 0-9727954-0-5 paperback

Printing & Importing info@PirsumInc.com
Cover by Spotlight Design

Contents

Stories, Parables,
Anecdotes and Sayings

Insights

Foreword

Chicken Soup: The traditional, rich golden broth coveted by every generation. Like penicillin, it is a powerful remedy that cures all ailments. Several spoonfuls warm the body and the *neshama*, soul.

This can serve as an analogy for the effects of a potent and powerful story, parable, insight or saying.

Chassidim spread the Torah's teachings through story-telling, a universal language. A concise statement packs a wealth of meaning into a few, frugal words. A memorable quotation jump-starts the brain. It may capture the essence of a whole Torah lesson. A short story or one-liner can, when internalized, warm the body and soul.

This is the revised edition of the book that was originally distributed in honor of our wedding, 11 Tammuz, 5761 (July 2, 2001). It includes some of our favorite stories, insights, and sayings, containing life-long lessons.

These stories and quotations were collected and heard from the Rebbe, teachers, parents, family and friends. We also selected them from books, advertisements, classes, lectures, articles, e-mails, and even tea boxes. We threw in some original insights and observations as well.

Whenever possible, the source is acknowledged at the end of the story. A reference may indicate the individual from whom we heard the story, not the original author. For acknowledgments for previously published stories, please refer to the "Permissions" section at the end of this book.

Although we would like to credit each author, many of these stories have become part of us, and thus, by being told and retold, we have forgotten the source. We thank them for this, because more than being a source for the stories, they have become a source for the lessons!

The quotations following a story often complement the story's theme. Sometimes, however, they may offer a different insight.

These stories and insights contain broad implications. We have sorted them according to categories, yet they may have other implications. Sometimes morals are offered; others are left for the reader to draw his own conclusions.

Please don't understand this compilation as absolute truth; rather, consider it as a handy starting point. It is only a means to an end.

At a *farbrengen*, the Rebbe told a story of Rabbi Schneur Zalman of Liadi, the first Lubavitcher Rebbe. During the story, the Rebbe paused and said, "I have not heard this story from my father-in-law, so I cannot vouch for its authenticity. I assure you, though, that the moral of the story is true!"

The stories presented here stem from Chassidic teachings, true-life experiences, and fiction. The common denominator is the everlasting lessons they contain.

Someone once showed the Rebbe a book written by a German philosopher, in which the author explained that he reached the conclusion that every Jew has two souls.

The Rebbe commented, "Once Rabbi Schneur Zalman of Liadi revealed this in the *Tanya*, it has been revealed to the world, including this author." *(Kfar Chabad Magazine #917)*

Some of the stories, insights and quotes do not appear to stem from Chassidic sources. However, in reality, these thinkers found several good words to sum up a rich Chassidic concept...

❧

We fervently hope that the inspiration gained from these stories will inspire deeds of goodness and kindness – "the deed is the main thing" – that will usher in the arrival of *Moshiach!*

Pesach & Chana

Acknowledgments

We wish to express our gratitude to the Rebbe, our parents and family, teachers, friends and study partners.

They have either shared these stories and lessons with us, or helped us develop the capacity to search out lessons on our own and share their meaning with others.

Special thanks to: Tzvi Burston for contributing the majority of the typing. To Moshe Muchnik, of Spotlight Design, for the cover design. To Rabbi Mendel Lifshitz for the glossary. To Yossi Mizrachi, Yehoshofot Oliver, Mrs. Yehudis Cohen and Rivky Brenenson for editorial assistance. Rabbi Michoel A. Seligson and Rabbi Yosef Y. Keller for assistance in finding sources. A special thank you to Rabbi Levi Wineberg for reviewing the content.

We would like to acknowledge those who have stories printed in their names. (Note: The stories and sayings that were penned anonymously, that are public domain, whose authors are unknown, or that were written by Pesach and Chana Burston, are not included in this listing. For previously published materials, please see "Permissions" at the end of this book):

Rabbi Chaim Bryski, Rabbi Chaim Binyomin Burston, Tzvi Burston, Rabbi Tzemach Cunin, Rabbi Adin Even-Yisroel (Stiensaltz), Rabbi Yossi Goldman, Rabbi Yossi Goldstein ("Uncle Yossi"), Rabbi Menachem Mendel Gordon, Rabbi Yisroel Gordon, Rabbi Yossi Greenberg, Rabbi Dovid Hazdan, Rabbi Moshe Herson, Rabbi Asher Herson, Mrs. Rochel Holtzkenner, Rabbi Yosef Y. Jacobson, Rabbi Yosef Konikov, Rabbi Yehuda Krinsky, Rabbi Shloma

Majeski, Yossi Mizrachi, Rabbi Zevi Raskin, Rabbi Akiva Wagner, Rabbi Yehoshua Werde, Rabbi Levy Wineberg and Rabbi Shloima Zarchi.

Any oversights discovered will be corrected in future editions.

Most of all we'd like to thank you, dear reader, for tasting this chicken soup and passing it on; for keeping that traditional chicken soup alive.

Stories, Parables,
Anecdotes and Sayings

(Dis)Ability

In Brooklyn, New York, Chush is a school that caters to learning-disabled children. At a Chush fundraising dinner, the father of a Chush child delivered an unforgettable speech.

After extolling the school and its dedicated staff, he cried out, "Where is the perfection in my son Shaya? Everything G-d does is done with perfection. But my child cannot understand things as other children do. He cannot remember facts and figures as other children do.   Where is G-d's perfection?"

The audience was shocked by the question, pained by the father's anguish and stilled by the piercing query. "I believe," the father answered, "that when G-d brings a child like this into the world, the perfection that he seeks is in the way people react to this child."

He then related the following story about his son Shaya:

One afternoon Shaya and his father walked past a park where some boys they knew were playing baseball. Shaya asked, "Do you think they will let me play?"

Shaya's father knew his son was not at all athletic and that most boys would not want him on their team. But Shaya's father understood that if his son were chosen to play it would give him a sense of belonging.

Shaya's father approached one of the boys in the field and asked if Shaya could play. The boy looked around for reassurance from his teammates. Getting none, he took matters into his own hands and said, "We are losing by six runs and the game is in the eighth inning. I guess he can be on our team and we'll try to put him up at bat in the ninth inning."

Shaya's father was ecstatic as his son smiled broadly. Shaya was told to put on a glove and go out to play short center field. In the bottom of the eighth inning, Shaya's team scored a few runs, but was still behind by three. In the bottom of the ninth inning, Shaya's team scored again. Now there were two outs and the bases were loaded. With the potential winning run on base, Shaya was scheduled to be up at bat.

Would the team actually let Shaya bat at this juncture and give away their chance to win the game? Surprisingly, Shaya was given the bat. Everyone knew it was all but impossible to win because Shaya didn't even know how to hold the bat properly, let alone hit with it. As Shaya stepped up to the plate, the pitcher moved a few steps forward to lob the ball in softly so Shaya could at least make contact. When the first pitch came in, Shaya swung clumsily and missed.

One of the other boys approached Shaya and together they held the bat and faced the pitcher, waiting for the next pitch. The pitcher again took a few steps forward to toss the ball softly toward Shaya. As the pitch came in, they swung the bat together, and hit a slow ground ball to the pitcher. The pitcher picked up the soft grounder and could have easily thrown the ball to the first basemen. Shaya would have been out, ending the game. Instead, the pitcher took the ball and threw it in a high arc to the right field, far beyond reach of the first basemen.

Everyone started yelling, "Shaya, run to first! Run to first!" Never in his life had Shaya run to first. He scampered down the baseline wide-eyed and startled. By the time he reached first base, the right fielder had the ball. He could have thrown the ball to the second baseman, and tag out Shaya, who was still running. But the right fielder understood the pitcher's intentions, and threw the ball high and far over the third basemen's head. Everyone yelled, "Run to second, run to second!"

Shaya ran towards second base as the runners ahead of him deliriously circled the bases towards home. As Shaya reached second base, the opposing shortstop ran to him, turned him in the direction of third base and shouted, "Run to third!" As Shaya rounded third, the boys from both teams ran behind him screaming, "Shaya run home!" Shaya ran home, stepped on plate and all eighteen boys lifted him on their shoulders and made him the hero, as he had just hit a 'grand slam' and won the game for his team.

"That day," said the father softly with tears rolling down his face, "those eighteen boys reached their level of G-d's perfection."

–*From Rabbi Pesach Krohn*

"Disability: Why focus on the 'dis'
when you can focus on the 'ability'?"
—Tzvi Burston

"People with special needs reveal what is special in us."

"Don't let the things you can't do
get in the way of the things you can."

Accomplishment

A criminal was sentenced to ten years of prison. His daily job demanded him to turn a lever bolted into the back wall. He imagined that a flourmill was attached to the lever on the other side of the wall.

Thinking how fortunate he was to be productive while imprisoned helped him remain sane. As he turned the lever, he would reflect at how much he was accomplishing. He imagined the bakers gathering his fine flour, and kneading it into dough to make fresh bread for the townspeople. This thought filled his life with purpose.

After ten years, upon release, the man was eager to taste of the bread, the fruit of his hard labor for so many years. With mighty strides he headed for the mill. But alas, as the man turned the corner, he fell to the ground in a faint.

There was nothing at the other side of the wall.

–Heard from Rabbi Chaim Binyomin Burston, adapted from the Midrash

"Do not mistake activity for achievement."

"Talent without discipline is like an octopus on roller skates: There's plenty of movement, but you never know if it will be forward, backwards or sideways."

Answer

Duvy beamed with pride as he jumped up and down with his treasured prize. Up and down, higher and higher he jumped on his trampoline, aiming to touch his new, shiny toy truck to the clouds. In a frenzy of excitement, the toy slipped out of his small hands and crashed onto the ground, shattering into a mess of broken pieces. Duvy was devastated. With thick, salty tears running down his tender cheeks, Duvy gazed toward the sky and prayed passionately to G-d to please put the pieces of his toy together again.

His big sister laughed at Duvy and mockingly asked, "My dear baby brother, do you really expect G-d to answer your prayers?"

"You will see that G-d will answer me," Duvy replied, with a twinkle of faith in his little brown eyes. His sister laughed and went into the house.

A few hours later, when the sister returned, she was not surprised to see the pieces of the shiny toy truck still strewn across the green grass. "Well Duvy, has G-d answered?" she asked.

"Yes," was Duvy's reply, "He said 'no.'"

*"Happiness is not an absence of problems,
but the ability to deal with them."*

Application

One of the greatest disciples of the Maggid of Mezritch, Reb Pinchas, had begun life like many of his contemporaries, far from the ways of Chassidism. When rumors reached his city concerning the new path of Divine service the Maggid was paving, Reb Pinchas was inspired to investigate.

Before he visited the Maggid, he prepared a difficult Talmudic question to ask him, through which he could test the Maggid's scholarship. When Reb Pinchas finally merited an audience with the Maggid, he did not get a chance to speak. The Maggid immediately told him, "I suggest you go speak to my pupil, Reb Zusia. You will surely benefit." Reb Pinchas was dismissed and went to meet Reb Zusia.

Reb Zusia did not look like much of a scholar. Most of the day he did not study, but sat and recited *Psalms*. When Reb Pinchas asked Reb Zusia to learn with him, Reb Zusia replied that he was incapable of teaching the scholar. "However," Reb Zusia said, "I have a Torah question that perhaps you might help me with."

Reb Zusia brought out a volume of the *Talmud* and, opening to a certain page, he read aloud, "Rav Huna said: 'Nine can combine with an Ark.' If there are only nine Jews and a *minyan* is needed, the Ark may be counted as the tenth person. The *Talmud* asks: 'But is an Ark a person?' The *Talmud* then phrases the law differently.

"My question," Reb Zusia continued, "is as follows: Doesn't the *Talmud* already know that an Ark is not a person? What is the *Talmud* teaching us?"

Reb Pinchas was speechless. He had never encountered such an unusual question, so he turned to leave. Reb Zusia said, "Pardon me, Rabbi, but perhaps the *Talmud* is trying to impart a very important lesson indeed: A Jew must not think that just because he is an 'Ark full of Torah Scrolls' – he has learned much Torah – this automatically makes him a 'person.' In fact, it's quite possible that this 'case full of Torahs' may not be a 'person' at all.

"This is what we learn here in Mezritch," Reb Zusia concluded, "how to be a *mensch*, a 'person.' The objective is not only for a person to learn Torah, but to have the Torah teach one to be a 'person.'"

Reb Pinchas understood why he had come to Mezritch and what he had been missing. He remained in Mezritch and eventually became one of the Maggid's greatest disciples.

–Adapted from Rabbi J.J. Hecht

"Chassidus is Divine intelligence that shows man how small he is, and how great he can become."
— Hayom Yom, 19 Iyar

"People don't care how much you know until they know how much you care."

"To become different from what we are, we must know who we are."

Aspiration

The children gathered around the tree and commented to each other how high it was, and how exciting it would be to climb to the top. They opted to play a game to see who could climb to the top of the tree without falling. Among the participating children was five-year-old Menachem Mendel, the future Lubavitcher Rebbe. His mother, Rebbetzin Chana, observed the children as they played.

All the other boys succeeded, at best, to reach halfway up the tree before falling, while Menachem Mendel reached the top.

Later, his mother asked him, "Mendel, how did you succeed to reach the top when the other children failed?"

"It was easy," answered the child. "The other children kept looking down, and as soon as they realized how high they were, they became dizzy and fell. I, however, looked only upward. When I saw how low I was, I kept going higher and higher until I reached the top."

—Adapted from "Yimei Melech"

"A lesson from a bicycle:
One can only maintain balance by riding forward."
—Rabbi Dovid Hazdan

"When one is connected Above, one does not fall down below."
—Reb Meir of Premishlan

Assistance

A small boy was struggling to move a heavy wooden cupboard, but it would not budge. He pushed and shoved with every muscle in his body, but couldn't manage to move it even an inch! His father, passing by, stopped to watch his son's futile efforts. Finally the father asked, "Son, are you using all your strength?"

"Yes, I am!" the boy cried, exasperated.

"No," the father said calmly, "you're not. You have not asked me to help you."

"The next best thing to knowing something is knowing where to find it."

"To make an apple pie from scratch, you must first create the universe."

Assurance

Standing at the river's edge, a boy gazed serenely into the distance. A curious observer approached the child and inquired what he was waiting for.

Without hesitation the youth pointed toward the river and replied, "I am waiting for that steamboat to pick me up."

"Foolish boy," remarked the man, "boats don't stop everywhere. You must wait at the pier." The boy did not reply, and to the amazement of the stranger, the boat turned to pick up the youngster.

"You see," exclaimed the boy with confidence as he boarded the boat, "the captain is my father!"

Balance

"When I first arrived at *yeshiva*," recalls Tzvi Freeman, "I threw myself entirely into the experience. Soon I realized I had lost my balance. It was at that time I heard these words of the Rebbe, and they guided me:

"The *Talmud* relates: 'Four entered into the orchard (the mystical teachings). One died, one went mad, and one became a heretic. Rabbi Akiva entered in peace and left in peace.'

"Why was Rabbi Akiva capable of leaving in peace? Because he entered in peace; he had made peace between his physical and spiritual worlds, between his body and his soul, and saw purpose in them both.

"So when he entered the spiritual he had in mind his return to the physical. And when he re-entered the physical he brought with him the spiritual."

—From "Bringing Heaven Down to Earth"

"An animal walks with its face to the earth, for earthiness and materiality is all that it knows. Man walks upright, for man was born to gaze upon and aspire to the Heavens."
—Rabbi DovBer of Mezritch

Beginning Vs. Ending

After finally reaching the shores of America, a Russian immigrant searched for employment in order to support his family. He resolved to open a small shop. A friend advised him that in order to attract customers, he should advertise his shop by placing a catchy sign on the storefront. Following his friend's advice, he ordered a large sign that read, "Grand Opening," and affixed it for all to see.

The next day, the immigrant observed a significant crowd gathered around a particular shop. Taking a closer look at what was causing such an attraction, he noticed a bright-colored sign on the store window. Although he could not read English, he noticed that on this sign there were more words than he had on his shop's storefront. "I should get a sign just like that one," he thought to himself, as he carefully jotted down the words on a piece of paper. Immediately he ordered a sign to be ready the following day.

The next morning, adjacent to his "Grand Opening" sign he proudly affixed his new sign reading, "Going Out of Business."

"Some people are working backstage,
some are playing in the orchestra,
some are on stage singing,
some are in the audience as critics
and some are there to applaud.
Know who and where you are."

Belief

The subject of discussion was the idea of "belief verses reality." A secular educator in Communist Russia was teaching a science and ethics class to her young students. She began her lecture with the claim that whatever cannot be seen, does not exist.

"You know why you can't see a flying saucer in the sky?" the teacher asked her audience. "Because there isn't one! And for that same reason," she explained, "we all believe that there is no G-d in this world. We can't see Him; therefore He doesn't exist."

A witty student, sitting at the back corner of the room, raised his hand and blurted out, "Does that mean that the teacher has no brain? I mean, none of us can see it?!"

"To the believer there are no questions; to the skeptic there are no answers."

"The less one knows, the easier it is to convince him that he knows it all."

Blessing

Rabbi Elimelech, the Rabbi of Lizhensk, was widely recognized as a righteous, holy Jew and an accomplished scholar.

Once a young Torah scholar visited Rabbi Elimelech.

"Rabbi Elimelech," began the visitor, "we are both scholars, well-versed in Jewish law. Yet you have far surpassed me in your level of saintliness. What do you possess that I lack?"

Rabbi Elimelech pointed to the bowl of fruit displayed before them on the table. "When you want to eat an apple, do you make a blessing to G-d?"

"I certainly do!" the visiting rabbi answered.

"Ah – that's the difference! You see, when you want to eat an apple, you make a blessing. When I want to make a blessing, I eat an apple."

Comment:

When we bless a friend, we wish him success. Can we do the same towards G-d? Does G-d lack something that our prayers can satisfy?

This story illustrates that blessings allow us to become close to the Creator of the world. Not only do we thank G-d for His kindness by making a blessing, we are also elevated to a higher level of spiritual awareness.

The visiting rabbi used the blessing to thank G-d for His material blessings, which is commendable. But Rabbi Elimelech used the blessing to connect to G-d. The apple was merely a medium for this.

When the opportunity arises to make a blessing, we too can use it to increase our spiritual awareness. The more blessings that we make, the more we increase our awareness.

That's the point of making a blessing. It is as if we do something for G-d; we bring Him here on earth instead of relegating Him to the heavens.

Challenge

The Rebbe once sent a *shliach* on a specific mission. Upon his return, the *shliach* reported to the Rebbe that although the mission had been extremely challenging, he performed his task successfully.

The Rebbe looked at the chassid and responded, "Since when have you made a contract with G-d that everything is easy?"

–Heard from Rabbi Menachem M. Gordon

"There can be no victories without battle,
no peaks without valleys
and no roses without thorns."

"Never fear shadows –
it means that there's light nearby."

"Sometimes we must go backwards to go forward."

"Don't be discouraged –
it may be the last key in the bunch that opens the door."

Choice

A young skeptic, wishing to test the wisdom of a seer, held his closed fist before the venerated man.

"What have I in my hand?" the youth asked.

"A butterfly," was the answer.

"Is it alive or dead?" queried the youth.

The old man knew that the youth was sporting with him. If he replied dead, the youth would open his hand and let the butterfly fly away. If he replied alive, the youth would close his fist and crush the creature.

The seer replied, "It is in your hands – whatever you wish to make if it."

–Heard at a Bar-Mitzva in South Africa

*"Whether you think that you can, or that you can't –
you are usually right."*

*"When every other element is out of your control,
remember that you can still manage your reaction."*

*"Money is fire. It can destroy and annihilate, or illuminate and
warm, depending on how it is used."*
—Rabbi Elimelech of Lizensk

Citizen Vs. Tourist

It was a chilly winter night in the early 1940s, and the Academic Principal of the Rabbinical College at 770, Lubavitch World Headquarters, prepared to return home after a long day of instructing his students. As the Principal was not a Lubavitcher chassid, he did not usually attend the Chassidic gatherings that transpired among the young men.

However, that night, he noticed that the students were *farbrenging* with vigor. He inquired what event had inspired this gathering, and was told that it was the famous holiday of the first Lubavitcher Rebbe's liberation, *Yud-Tes Kislev*. Once he was there, the Principal granted the students' request that he speak.

The Principal sat among the students, accepted a small cup of vodka to say "*L'chaim,*" and said, "In every country there are citizens and there are tourists. The difference is that a citizen is deeply committed to his country. He cares about improving its cleanliness, voting for worthy leaders, and the like. Tourists lack this sense of loyalty."

Then, raising his cup, he exclaimed, "*L'chaim* – you boys should be 'citizens' of Judaism, not 'tourists!'"

–Heard from Rabbi Levi Wineberg

"It's better to be on the outside looking in,
than on the inside looking out."
—Adapted from Rabbi Yosef Yitzchok of Lubavitch

Common Sense

A chassid wrote to the Rebbe complaining that he had experienced a series of thefts in his Crown Heights home.

"Perhaps I should have my *mezuzos* checked?" he suggested.

"Perhaps you should check the security of your windows," was the Rebbe's reply.

—*Souvenir Journal, 15 Elul 5758, South Africa*

"Ask advice, but use common sense."

"It is unfortunate to have more dollars than sense."

Compassion

Rabbi Akiva, the renowned Talmudic sage, prepared for his lovely daughter's wedding with mixed emotions. Although he eagerly awaited the special day, anxiety enveloped his heart. Many years earlier, pagan astrologers had predicted that a poisonous snake would bite his daughter on her wedding day. He resolved not to relay his fears to anyone, and to trust in G-d that his daughter would be safe.

The wedding day arrived, and the guests ate and danced joyfully. In the midst of the celebration, a hungry beggar entered the hall and stared at the banquet of scrumptious food. He pleaded for food, but no one noticed him.

Only the bride saw the poor man. She quietly took her plate of food and gave it to him. No one noticed her act of kindness, and no one realized that the bride herself had not eaten.

That evening, Rabbi Akiva's daughter retreated to her room. She removed the large gold pin that had secured her veil and stuck it in a crack between the tiles of the wall.

The bride awoke the next morning and was shocked to find a dead snake stuck beneath her gold pin. The snake had been hiding, waiting to bite the bride. She had killed the snake unintentionally with her golden pin.

When Rabbi Akiva heard of the incident, he remembered the words of the pagan astrologers.

"Tell me, dear daughter, what special deed did you do yesterday to deserve G-d's mercy?"

His daughter recounted her act of kindness, and Rabbi Akiva exclaimed, "For the act of giving charity, G-d spared your life! May you perform many more good deeds..."

Comment:

It is when we become self-absorbed, whether in our own moments of joy or, G-d forbid, sorrow, that we may forget to fulfill the needs of others. Rabbi Akiva's daughter demonstrates that one must always be sensitive to another...

"We exist temporarily through what we take, but we live forever through what we give."

Compromise

A group of experienced architects were studying architecture in London. Upon visiting "Big Ben," one architect questioned the other, "Why is the clock so high? It is most inconvenient. If I were inside a car, it would be very difficult to tell the time!"

His companion explained, "Years ago, the clock was much lower. But its height had to be changed. You see, whenever someone stood by the clock, they would glance at their own watch, and then at the big clock. When they found that their time differed from Ben's, they would adjust Ben! Eventually, after so many adjustments, the clock broke.

"Now," concluded the architect, "everyone must adjust their watches to what is 'high' rather than adjusting what is 'high' to match what is 'below.'"

–Heard from Yosef Konikov

"Shoot for 100 and you may reach 80.
But shoot for 80 and you certainly won't reach 100."

Concentration

"One must speak and learn *Chassidus* even while busy working in mundane affairs," Rabbi Shmuel of Lubavitch demanded of his chassidim.

"How is it possible to think about concepts of *Chassidus* while we are busy from head to toe in business?" a chassid once lamented to the Rebbe in a private audience.

"If it is possible to think about business while you are praying, it is also possible for you to think about *Chassidus* while you are working!" was the Rebbe's reply.

–From "Sipurei Chassidim, Festivals," story 357

"Where your thoughts are, you are – in your entirety."
—Rabbi Yisroel Baal Shem Tov

Confession

With great remorse, a man entered the private room of Rabbi Shmuel of Lubavitch to ask for a formula for repentance. Since the man was ashamed to admit that he was the sinner, he explained that a friend had committed the sins and was too embarrassed to appear before the Rebbe personally. Therefore, his friend had asked him to come to the Rebbe on his behalf. Consequently, the visitor then gave the Rebbe a list of sins his "friend" had supposedly committed.

"What a fool the other man is," the Rebbe answered with a knowing smile, "he could have come himself and said that his friend sent him."

–Told by the Rebbe, 12 Tammuz 5714

"Many people, when they run into a pole, blame the pole."

"No man has a good enough memory to be a successful liar."
— Abraham Lincoln

*"When you tell the truth,
you need never worry about your lousy memory."*

Confidence

Once a father and son were traveling with their only donkey. The father rode on the donkey, and the son walked beside him. Upon reaching their first destination, the people of the city greeted them with nasty and crude remarks.

"Is this a father?" they shouted. "Would a responsible father ride his donkey while his son walks?" The father and son felt terribly embarrassed, so they continued traveling on to the next city. Before they entered, they switched places, hoping that the people of this city would be more accepting of them.

The travelers were again met with harsh criticism. "Look at this shameful sight! A disrespectful son rides on a donkey while his elderly father walks!" Feeling humiliated, the travelers left that city as well.

As they approached their third destination, the father suggested that they both ride on the donkey together. This would undoubtedly leave no room for insults.

As they neared the city, however, the people gathered to view the sight. "Look at that poor donkey!" they remarked. "It can barely walk due to the weight of those silly travelers! Why, it will be dead in no time!"

The father and son tried their luck one last time. The only option seemed to be that they both walk beside the donkey. As they entered the city, the donkey bolted and ran away. The people of the city watched in amusement and laughed mockingly. Rejected and hopeless, left with nothing, the travelers realized that efforts to please others will never succeed.

—Heard from Rabbi Shloma Majeski

Comment:

Acting to please others can never be successful. A person who wishes to impress others will have to constantly change, for every person will demand something different. We must act according to Torah values, without being influenced by others' views. Only this can bring a person to true satisfaction and joy.

"If I am I because I am I,
and you are you because you are you,
than I am I and you are you.
But if I am I because you are you,
and you are you because I am I,
then I am not I and you are not you."
—Reb Mendel of Kotzk

"If you don't stand for something, you'll fall for anything."

"The one who uses the loudest voice
usually has the weakest argument."

"The display of status-symbols is a result of low self-esteem.
The self-confident person projects a modest image."

"No one can make you feel inferior without your consent."

"Only the strongest of men are gentle."

Conformity

Several Bar-Mitzva age boys stopped attending Hebrew school. A concerned *shliach* took the teenagers to visit the Rebbe, hoping the Rebbe would convince them to continue seeking a Jewish education.

"Tell me," the Rebbe asked the first boy, "why have you decided to stop attending Hebrew school?"

"All the other boys on my block have stopped going to Hebrew school, so I want to stop as well," he answered.

"And what about you?" the Rebbe asked the second boy.

"Same reason," the boy explained, "the kids on my block don't go, so why should I?"

"Tell me," the Rebbe asked the boys, "who were your favorite Jewish heroes that you learned about?"

One boy responded that he deeply admired Noah, and the other, Abraham.

"Do you know," the Rebbe told the first boy, "that if Noah would have followed all the other kids on his block, we would have no world? And if Abraham would have followed all the kids on his block," the Rebbe told the second boy, "we would have no Jewish people!"

"Stick up for what's right, even if you'll stick out."

Connection

Yossi, the Bar-Mitzva boy, eagerly unwrapped his Bar-Mitzva presents. Living in the 21st century, it was not surprising that one of his relatives gave him a fancy new cell phone!

"How is it possible," he asked his father, admiring the wireless phone he held in his hands, "to have a phone that works without wires attached?"

His wise father answered, "So tell me, Yossi, you'd be able to understand how it works *with* wires?!"

Comment:

Naturally, our psyche allows us to think that we can connect to something solely when we can visualize and comprehend the connection.

In the case of a telephone, visible wires indicate the channel through which the connection travels. It seems simple, but in reality, we don't understand the connection via wires either, it's only that our psyche thinks it makes sense. We only begin to have questions when we see a cellular phone, which has no wires visibly making a connection.

Our understanding of *hiskashrus*, how we connect to the Rebbe, is similar to Yossi and the way he related to his cell phone.

Even when we were able to physically see the Rebbe, while we had a seemingly "wired" connection, we thought we understood. It may have seemed clear how we were able to connect to the Rebbe.

However, when the Rebbe was physically taken from us, it became a "cellular" connection. Suddenly, questions arose and we began to wonder.

In essence, we didn't understand how the wires worked either. For our connection to the Rebbe is a spiritual one. Just as the Rebbe connected to us before, he connects to us now.

Be it via wires or wireless.

"Ask not what the Rebbe can do for you;
Ask what can you do for the Rebbe."

"Indeed, the Rebbe is with us.
But are we with the Rebbe?"

Conscience

A poor farmer desired to steal corn from his neighbor's field. He took his young son along with him to be the lookout. Before the father began, he carefully observed his surroundings, looking in every direction to ensure the coast was clear. Seeing that he was safe, he was just about to fill his bag with fresh, golden corn, when his son cried out, "Father, there is someone watching!" The father panicked, grabbed his son's hand, and they quickly left the field.

Once they arrived in neutral territory, the father glanced back to see who had almost caught him. "Where is there someone watching?" questioned the father, as no one was in sight.

"G-d is watching!" the son answered.

The father, conscience-stricken, took his boy by the hand and hurried home without the stolen corn.

"You can't fool G-d, and you can't fool other people. The only one you can fool is yourself. And what is the achievement of fooling a fool?"
—Rabbi Shmuel of Lubavitch

"Don't use an excuse you wouldn't put on paper."

Continuity

A large family walked home from synagogue contentedly on a sunny *Shabbos* afternoon. Without warning, an anti-Semite confronted them. "What business do you have raising such a large family?" he rudely shouted to the father. "It is very irresponsible! Can you provide for them? Are you able to devote enough time to each of your children?"

The father, unfazed by the man's insolence, calmly replied, "After I have six million children – you can ask me that question."

"If a Jew wishes to see a miracle today,
he need only look at himself.
The greatest of all miracles is
that even one Jew exists in our day and age."
—R. Bachya Ibn Paqua

"Living well really is the best revenge.
Being miserable because of a sour or past relationship
just might mean that the other person was right about you."

Contribution

News arrived in a town of wine-merchants that in two weeks the king was due to make his annual visit for inspection. The mayor instantly called an emergency meeting in the town square, and attendance was compulsory. As the masses filled the square, the mayor stepped up to the platform and began his speech:

"A short time remains until the king's arrival, and we must work quickly. In addition to individual preparations, such as cleaning our homes and preparing personal gifts, one general gift will be presented on behalf of the entire town. Every family is ordered to donate one cup of the finest wine to a golden casket that will be set up in the town square."

The crowd scurried away to carry out the mayor's instructions.

One couple began discussing the issue of the wine donation. They decided that if each townsman contributes a cup of wine to the casket, and they brought a single cup of water instead of wine, surly no one would realize. So why waste the expensive wine?

Late that night when no one was out, the husband tiptoed down the street and poured a cup of water into the casket. Little did he know that another townsman had shared his brilliant brainstorm, and so had another...

The big day arrived, at last, and everyone arrived in his finest attire to greet the king. The king sat on the golden throne built especially for him, and the mayor rose to speak. The mayor expressed feelings of honor and admiration for the king on behalf of the townspeople. As a token of appreciation he offered the king the magnificent golden casket, filled with rich wine.

As a sample, the mayor's attendant filled a golden goblet for the king to taste. To his astonishment, the attendant bent down and turned the faucet, only to see water!

–Heard from "Uncle Yossi"

"Details do make a difference."

"Sometimes, when I consider what tremendous consequences result from little things, I am tempted to think that there are no little things."

Creativity

A famous concert violinist enters the stage to perform a solo at a hall in New York City. Getting on stage is no small achievement for him. He was stricken with polio as a child, and has braces on both legs and walks with two crutches.

To see him walk across the stage, one step at a time, is an unforgettable sight. He walks painfully, yet majestically, until he reaches his chair. He sits down slowly, lays his crutches on the floor, undoes the clasps on his legs, tucks one foot back and extends the other foot forward. Then he bends down and picks up the violin, puts it under his chin, nods to the conductor and proceeds to play.

The audience sits reverently as he makes his way across the stage to his chair, undoes the clasps on his legs, and begins to play. But this time, something goes wrong. As he finishes the first few bars, one of the strings on his violin breaks. I can hear it snap – it resounds like gunfire across the room. There is no mistaking what that sound means. There is no mistaking what he must do.

Everyone thinks to himself: "He will have to get up, put on the clasps again, pick up the crutches and limp his way offstage – to find another string or another violin." But he doesn't. Instead, he pauses, shuts his eyes and signals the conductor to continue. The orchestra begins, and he plays from where he left off. And he plays with a passion, power and purity that the audience has never heard.

Of course, everyone knows that it is impossible to play a symphonic work with only three strings. I know that, and you know that, but tonight, this musician refuses to know that. You can see him modulating, changing, and recomposing the piece in his head. He seems to be re-tuning the strings to produce sounds that they have never made.

When he finishes, the room is filled with an awed silence. And suddenly, every corner of the auditorium bursts out in applause. They are on their feet, screaming and cheering, doing everything to show how much they appreciate his performance.

He smiles, wipes the sweat from this brow, raises his bow to quiet us, and then says, not boastfully, but in a quiet, pensive tone, "You know, sometimes it is the musician's task to find out how much music he can make with what is left."

What a powerful line that is. It has lingered in my mind ever since. Who knows? Perhaps this episode portrays an attitude about life – not just for musicians, but also for us all.

Perhaps our task in this unstable, fast-changing, bewildering world is to make music, at first with all that we have, and then, when that is no longer possible, with whatever we have left.

"Words are the pen of the heart; music is the pen of the soul."
—Rabbi Schneur Zalman of Liadi

"Never tell people how to do things. Tell them what to do – they will surprise you with their ingenuity."

Credit

It was the most significant business meeting of the year, and the businessman hoped to arrive early. When he entered the parking lot, he was distraught to discover that every spot was taken! He circled the parking lot frantically, hoping that someone would pull out.

"Dear G-d," he pleaded, "if You provide me with a parking space, I will give You 25% of my earnings." Despite his prayers, time continued to pass but he still could not locate a parking space.

Three minutes before the meeting, he cried out, "Dear G-d if You will find me a parking space I will give You 50% of my earnings!" The businessman's fortune did not seem to change.

"Okay G-d. The meeting is beginning in two minutes," the man exclaimed in desperation. "Help me and I will give You 75% of my earnings!" As he finished uttering his vow, a car pulled out of the parking spot closest to the door.

"G-d," said the businessman, "forget the deal. I found a parking spot."

"We ask G-d to provide for our needs, and then congratulate ourselves on our ability and cleverness."

"Harmony seldom makes a headline."

Criticism

A respectable and distinguished woman was horrified by her next-door neighbor's lifestyle. The neighbor seemed to be a horrendously poor housekeeper; she lived in a filthy house and raised messy, dirty children. The situation was disgraceful.

The woman decided to share her feelings of frustration with a visiting friend. "Just look at those clothes she has out on the line," she began, pointing to her neighbor's backyard. "See the black streaks spattered up and down those sheets and pillowcases?"

"It appears to be, my dear," answered the visitor, "that the clothes are perfectly clean. The streaks that you see are on your own window."

"Before you criticize someone, put yourself on the receiving end."

"When I start to find fault with all that I see,
it's time to start looking for what's wrong with me."
—Adapted from Rabbi Yisroel Baal Shem Tov

"When an archer misses the mark, he should look for the fault
within himself. Failure to hit the bull's-eye is never the fault
of the target. To improve your aim, improve yourself."

"When you point your finger at someone else,
three fingers are pointing at yourself."

Desire

Once, while hunting in the forest, a prince noticed a lovely child in the distance playing a heartwarming melody on a silver flute. The prince laid his rifle down and sat on a tree stump to let the pleasant melody saturate his soul.

Suddenly the music ceased, and the mesmerized prince dashed to find the child and hear this enchanting melody once more. He searched the entire forest, but the child was nowhere to be found.

The prince's heart yearned deeply for this sweet melody and he spent the rest of his days searching for this special tune.

–The Midrash

Comment:

Embedded deeply in the Jewish soul lies an unquenchable thirst for the precious music of Torah and its commandments; for fulfillment and spirituality. Our souls search for this melody that we naturally desire.

"Where a lantern is placed,
those who seek light gather around – for light attracts."
—Hayom Yom, 13 Teves

"Many things capture our eyes;
only a few should capture our heart."

Divine Providence

"If I stand in the street and get hit by a car, is that an act of Divine Providence?" a man asked his rabbi, inquiring about the topic of Divine Providence.

The rabbi explained, "A person was, by Divine Providence, given a brain and the ability to use it. Therefore, he should try to do his utmost not to get hit by a car. Hopefully, by Divine Providence, he won't get hit.

"However," the rabbi concluded, "if, for one reason or another, regardless of whether he tried to prevent it, the person gets hit, then yes – that is an act of Divine Providence."

Comment:

The concept of Divine Providence can be applied to both discovering one's unique life mission and finding one's destined mate: Are we supposed to make an effort to obtain the right mission or the desirable soul mate? If it is by Divine Providence, then perhaps we should suffice with praying, and let life take its course?

This story illustrates a powerful lesson: Yes, we should "pull strings" to find a preferred *shlichus* or a soul mate. But once we find ourselves in a certain place, or married to a certain person, we must believe that it is by Divine Providence.

"Make a plan."
—South African saying

Effect

The sand sparkled in the sunlight along the ocean shore. Scattered along the beach were thousands of starfish, dehydrating in the afternoon heat. A little boy walked along the shore, picking up each starfish and gently tossing it into the sea.

An old man watched the child's actions in dismay. He ran to the boy and asked, "Why are you bothering? Look how many thousands of starfish are scattered along the sand! Do you really think you are making a difference?"

The young boy reached down and picked up a starfish, and with pride he tossed it into the ocean. "I just made a world of a difference to that one!"

"Whoever preserves a single life from Israel is considered by Scripture as if he has preserved an entire world."
—Talmud, Sanhedrin 37b (in the Mishnah)

*"Each person is a whole world.
Do one person a favor and make a world of a difference."*

*"Work on making the world a better place –
one mitzva at a time."*

*"There are no unimportant jobs, no unimportant people
and no unimportant acts of kindness."*

Effort

"Why do a *mitzva* if I know I will sin afterward?"

A visitor once asked this blunt question to the Rebbe in a private audience. He understood that performing a good deed is meaningful, but thought that any merits gained would be wiped away upon sinning.

"Imagine a breathtaking scenic landmark," the Rebbe began. "A tourist captures the view with a photograph, and frames it beautifully. How much would the photograph sell for?" the Rebbe asked.

The man answered hesitantly, "About twenty-five dollars?"

The Rebbe continued his metaphor: "Another tourist who is an accomplished artist sees this magnificent sight and skillfully paints the scene. How much would his original artwork sell for?"

"Oh, it could be several thousand dollars!" exclaimed the man.

"Logically," the Rebbe explained, "the painting, despite its beauty, only captured several of the many details in the entire scene. The photograph, on the other hand, captured every detail of the landmark.

"Why is the painting worth more than the photograph?" the Rebbe asked.

The man, comprehending the Rebbe's parable, quickly replied, "It's the effort that counts!"

"Exactly!" the Rebbe concluded. "Angels are picture-perfect. Though they do not sin their perfection does not require effort. Humans are imperfect. We may make occasional mistakes, but our effort is very precious to G-d."

—Heard from Yehoshua Werde

Comment:

Imagine waiting to watch a performance. You anticipate seeing actors, props, dancing, and hearing lively music. But all you see before you is a curtain.

The curtain parts and everything is all there! Did it happen instantly? Of course not! The curtain revealed the culmination of weeks of preparation.

People may wonder, "Is *Moshiach* really going to appear suddenly? How could such a drastic change occur?"

The revelations of *Moshiach* will not happen instantly. Every good deed that has been done from the beginning of creation has been saved; frozen in the cosmos. When one commits sins, it may have a negative effect, yet it does not wipe away the good.

When *Moshiach* is revealed, it will be like a curtain that has just been opened.

"Today will never happen again.
But one good deed can make it last forever."

"The total is greater than the sum of its parts."

Enemies

President Abraham Lincoln was once criticized for his policy toward his enemies.

"Why do you try to befriend them?" he was asked. "You should try to destroy them."

"Do I not destroy my enemies," the President asked, "by befriending them?"

"In difficulty lies opportunity."
— Albert Einstein

"A lesson from film developing:
From one negative you can make countless positives."

"Give a man money and you help him for a day;
Teach him how to make money and you help him for a lifetime."
—Adapted from Maimonides

"You can't get rid of your temper by losing it."

Essence

"This is how the Rebbe greeted me as I entered a private audience," Rabbi Nachman Bernhard exclaimed as he pointed to a photo of the Rebbe smiling. A renowned *shliach* in South Africa, Rabbi Bernhard related some of his experiences with the Rebbe to his listeners.

"When it was announced that the Rebbe would no longer receive people for private audiences, I wrote a letter to the Rebbe conveying my feelings: Scientists expect that at the turn of the century a new pill will be invented. This pill will include all the nutrition included in an ordinary meal. One will no longer need to eat. It will provide all the essential vitamins and minerals. Additionally, this pill will be more beneficial than a meal, because it will eliminate all unnecessary and harmful ingredients.

"However, taking a pill cannot compare to eating an actual meal.

"Similarly, although the Rebbe is not offering private audiences, the Rebbe can surely accomplish just as much without these private sessions. But it just isn't the same..."

Comment:

Gimmel Tammuz presents a difficult challenge for chassidim. Our corporeal limitations impede our perception and we cannot physically see the Rebbe. However, we must be confident that the Rebbe is still with us. He is no longer confined by physical barriers and thus reveals himself to us through higher revelations than in the past.

But it just isn't the same... We don't see that smile...

We pray and demand to *see* the Rebbe again.

"Mind the gap."
—Announcement at the London underground system

Sometimes the deepest thoughts come from the innocent mouths of children. Here are several which the child within us can certainly appreciate:

- *Thinking about getting a shot is worse than getting one.*

- *By hitting the kid with the ball you might get the ball, but you won't have anyone to throw it to.*

- *If you wait until you are really sure, you'll never take off the training wheels.*

- *You need a little push to go down the big slide.*

- *If you hesitate to get your net, the butterfly will fly away.*

- *When you're dressed up like a princess, it's easier to act like one.*

- *You can't know if someone is looking at you, unless you are looking at them.*

Example

Snow and wind blew wildly on a white, winter day. Despite the dangerous weather conditions, a villager decided to visit a friend in the next village. The friend lived beyond a steep and rugged mountain. The villager had climbed the dangerous trail for several minutes, plowed through the drifts of snow and along the edge of a precipice, when he heard a soft voice call out, "Be careful, father, I'm walking in your steps."

"You can't go everywhere your kids go
– but your words can."
—Anti-smoking ad

"We teach what we know, but we reproduce what we are."

"Imitation is the best compliment."

"It's not what you are that counts. It's who you are."

Expectations

The man whispered, "G-d, speak to me," and a meadowlark sang. But the man did not hear.

So the man yelled, "G-d, speak to me!" And the thunder rolled across the sky. The man still did not listen.

He looked around and said, "G-d, let me see You." And a star shone brightly. But the man did not notice.

He shouted, "G-d, show me a miracle!" And a life was born. But the man did not know.

The man cried out in despair, "Touch me, G-d, and let me know You are here!" whereupon G-d reached down and touched the man. But the man brushed the butterfly away and walked on.

Comment:

Don't reject a blessing because it isn't packaged as you expect.

"Success is relative to expectations."

"Most people are as happy as they make up their minds to be."
— Abraham Lincoln

Faith

Once a man dreamed that he was walking along the beach with G-d. Across the sky flashed scenes from his life. For each scene, he noticed two sets of footprints in the sand: one belonging to him, and the other to G-d.

When the last scene of his life flashed before him, he looked back at the footprints in the sand. He noticed that along the path of his life, there was only one set of footprints. He also noticed that it happened at the lowest and saddest times.

This bothered him and he questioned G-d about it. "G-d, you said that once I decided to follow You, You'd walk with me all the way. But I see that during the most troublesome times in my life, there is only one set of footprints. How could You leave me when I needed You most?"

G-d replied, "My precious, precious child, I love you and would never leave you. During your times of trial and suffering I was carrying you."

Comment:

In the story of the Jewish people's exodus from Egypt, the Torah tells of the Jews' challenge to G-d: "Is G-d in our midst?" The subsequent passage recounts Amalek's attack on the Jewish nation.

Rashi (Exodus, 17:7-8), based on the *Midrash*, explains the juxtaposition of these two episodes: The very fact that the Jewish people questioned G-d's presence caused the difficulties. Had they realized that G-d was carrying them all along, G-d would never have permitted such an attack on His people.

Furthermore, the knowledge that G-d is carrying and guiding us brings fulfillment to the arduous journey.

Had the dreaming man realized that it was G-d Who was carrying him, it would not have been so difficult.

"Nostalgia is the realization that things weren't as unbearable as they seemed at the time."

Fear

Night after night, a young girl from a needy family would cry out in fear from nightmares. Her parents consulted their rabbi who said, "The Sages say that we dream at night what we think about during the day. Ask your daughter what she is afraid of."

When they asked her, she replied, "I often see how you both sit and worry over the poverty we live in. Of everything, I am most afraid of your fear."

–Adapted from "Toward a Meaningful Life"

"A brave man is not one who is not afraid,
but one whose will is stronger than his fear."

"Never let the fear of striking out get in your way."
—Babe Ruth

"If you never fail,
you're not taking enough risks."

Focus

"At the beginning of the Rebbe's leadership," recalls Rabbi Yehuda Krinsky, one of the Rebbe's secretaries, "the Rebbe called me into his room. He gave me two pages written by his holy hand and directed me to type them. The pages had writing on all sides, and arrows in all directions.

"This was the beginning of my job as the Rebbe's secretary, and I was overwhelmed. My feelings were noticeable by my expression.

"The Rebbe saw this and instructed me, 'Don't be intimidated by the "scribbling." Take it word by word, line by line, and everything will come out as it is meant to.'

"This instruction," commented Rabbi Krinsky, "remained with me all my life and surely contains a lesson for us all.

"The events of this world arouse questions and doubts. Our job is not to be intimidated by the ways of the world. They are only tests.

"We must follow the teachings of our *Rebbeim*, 'word by word, line by line.' Then our questions will disappear and our doubts will vanish. The Rebbe's words will be realized, and eventually, everything will come out as it is meant to."

–Heard from Rabbi Yehuda Krinsky

"The quickest way to accomplish many tasks is to do one at a time."

Friendship

As a weary traveler made his way along a lonely road, he noticed a dry, shriveled leaf in his path. Picking it up, he was amazed at the delightful fragrance it exuded.

"Oh, you poor withered leaf," he exclaimed, "Where did you get this exquisite perfume?"

"For a long time I have lain in the company of a rose," was the reply.

"To have a friend, be a friend."

"He who helps others ascend climbs the highest."

"The best thing to do behind a person's back – is pat it!"

"Happiness multiplies by division."

"Love your neighbors, but don't pull the fence down."

"A true friend is someone who knows us – and still likes us."

Future

A ruthless fire spread through the town and destroyed the home of Reb DovBer, the Maggid of Mezritch. A child of eight years old, Reb DovBer tried to console his distraught mother.

"Why are you crying so much?" asked the child, "Should one cry because a house burned down?"

"No, my son," she replied, "I am not weeping for the loss of the house, but for the document containing our family tree that was in the house. That document traced our family back to Reb Yochanan HaSandler, a direct descendent of King David and a disciple of Rabbi Akiva."

"Don't worry, mother," the child answered, "I will start a new family tree."

—From Sipurei Chassidim, Parshas Vaeira

"The best way to predict the future is to create it."

"Inside each school are books, desks, blackboards, computers and the world's future."
—Posted in Cheder Menachem's teachers' lounge

G-d

A French astronomer announced, "I have swept the universe with my telescope, and I find no G-d."

A famous violinist responded to him, "That is as unreasonable as if I were to say, 'I have taken my violin apart, examined each piece with my microscope and find no music.'"

"Living in this world, we view the back of a master embroidery piece. Mismatched colored strings, knotted and twisted, overlap to form a warped pattern. But G-d views the other side. Colors blended in unity, each detail perfectly patterned forms a design of the highest quality."
—Chana Burston

Giving

Sitting in a Russian bar indulging in drinks, a group of friends enjoyed one another's company. They expressed their sincere love for the Czar and his domain.

Feeling overwhelmed with loyalty toward the Czar, one of the men proclaimed, "If I possessed a magnificent palace, I would dedicate it to the Czar!"

"Really?" his friends asked, looking impressed. "And what if you owned a fancy wagon with a herd of horses attached to it?"

"Yes, yes, for sure!" he answered.

"And if you owned a farm of animals?" they persisted.

"Yes again! For the Czar, his Majesty, I would give anything," the man declared confidently.

The other men doubted their friend, and assumed that the alcohol was taking its toll on his sanity. They challenged him further. "If you owned two chickens, would you give them to the Czar?"

The man became serious and quietly admitted, "No."

Perceiving the expressions of amazement on his friends' faces, the man honestly explained, "These are things I actually own."

–Heard from Rabbi Asher Herson

Goal

Exiled to Siberia, Reb Mendel Futerfas found himself in prison with a tightrope walker. Reb Mendel asked him, "I always wondered: You walk between such tall buildings – how do you maintain your balance?"

The tightrope walker answered, "It's simple. Before I begin, I find an object on the other end and focus on it. I don't dare take my eyes off the object while I'm walking. I don't look to the right; I don't look to the left. As long as I focus on my goal, I make it across."

Comment:

Be focused like the tightrope walker, or else you'll lose your footing.

"Obstacles are those frightful things you see when you take your eyes off the goal."

"You become successful the moment you start moving toward a successful goal."
—Bumper sticker

Gratitude

Chaim Moshe, the well to do merchant, was a pleasant fellow, but hated to pay the requested price for anything!

One day, while eating herring, a bone became lodged in his throat. He could neither swallow it nor disgorge it, and within moments he could scarcely breathe. His wife frantically called the family doctor, who arrived as the patient's face was turning blue. The physician quickly removed the bone.

When Chaim Moshe recovered and was breathing normally, he was overwhelmed with gratitude, but cautiously asked, "How much do I owe you for this quick procedure?"

The doctor was well acquainted with the merchant's miserly nature. "I'll tell you what," he said. "Just pay me half of what you would have paid when the bone was stuck in your throat!"

"Ask not, 'How can I get all the things I want?'
Ask, 'How can I enjoy the things I have?'"

Harmony

With patience and wisdom, a teacher instructed his young student in the reading of the Torah.

The teacher explained, "When you see two 'yuds' together in the text, do not read the word as it appears. This is G-d's holy name. Rather, say 'Hashem,' meaning 'the name of G-d.'

With new understanding, the boy attempted to read the verses. At the conclusion of each verse, the teacher was puzzled to hear the child say, "Hashem."

"Where do you see G-d's name after every verse?" the teacher asked.

The child pointed to the two dots at the end of every verse. These dots stand one above the other, like a colin, and are used to separate the verses.

The teacher smiled. "Dear child, a Jew is represented by the letter 'yud.' When two 'yuds' stand side by side, in unity, G-d is happy and dwells there. These are the two 'yuds' that are pronounced as G-d's name.

"But if one Jew stands above another, and they are not in harmony, G-d does not dwell there. These are the two 'yuds' at the end of each verse; they represent the end, not G-d's holy name."

"In Noah's ark the wolf lay next to the lamb,
but did not become a lamb.
Peace is when different opinions can coexist."

Incentive

The Chassidic town of Dokshitz held a weekly get-together for its residents. A samovar of *pannes* – a hot drink made with boiling water, vodka and sugar – was served to the participants. Reb Aryeh, the *mashpia* of Dokshitz, would teach a class in deep Chassidic thought from the book *Torah Ohr*.

Their Rebbe, Rabbi Shmuel of Lubavitch, didn't like this idea. "*Torah Ohr* combined with *pannes*?" he asked Reb Aryeh when he heard how the sublime 'soul of Torah' was perused in Dokshitz. "Tell me, what is the connection between a Chassidic discourse and a glass of *pannes*?"

The next time that Reb Aryeh was in the town of Lubavitch, the Rebbe inquired about the class. The *mashpia* was forced to report that participation in the weekly study group had steadily dwindled since the *pannes* had been eliminated from the program. "Nu," said the Rebbe, "bring back the *pannes*. As long as they study *Torah Ohr*..."

–From "Chabad Online Weekly Magazine"

"Choose a job you love;
you will never have to work a day in your life."

Individuality

It was *Rosh Hashana* eve, and hundreds of Jews stood in line to give letters of requests for blessings to the Rebbe. As the line progressed, a *yeshiva* student turned to a *shliach* near him asking about the blessing "may you be written and inscribed for a good year" that the Rebbe was then conveying to each person:

"How can this 'standard' blessing be intended specifically for me?" he asked.

The *shliach* gently explained, "An average person is indeed incapable of bestowing a communal blessing individually. But the Rebbe is different. He is *your* Rebbe," the *shliach* said with assurance. "Although you are one of thousands of black hats standing in line, he knows you personally and showers his blessings upon you. This is the Rebbe's greatness."

When his turn arrived, the student handed his letter to the Rebbe, received the standard blessing, and turned to leave. But the Rebbe summoned him back. The Rebbe turned to the boy, stared deeply and knowingly into his eyes, and repeated, "May you be written and inscribed for a good year!"

"Birth is G-d's way of telling you: You matter."
—The Rebbe

"Many become leaders because
they brought others to believe in them.
The Rebbe is a great leader because he believes so much in us."
—From "Bringing Heaven Down To Earth"

Instant Gratification

A brutal Russian winter raged, and a chassid wished to teach his son the importance of immersion in the *mikva*. Father and son approached a frozen lake on the outskirts of the city. The chassid undressed his shivering son and broke a hole in the ice. "When you immerse, you will feel chilled," the father explained gently, "but afterward I will wrap you in a warm blanket."

The chassid dipped his child in the icy lake. As soon as the child's body touched the freezing lake, the child shrieked, "ooooh!" Immediately the father lifted his child out of the lake and wrapped him in a warm blanket. The child emitted a sigh of contentment, "ahhh."

"Throughout life," the chassid explained, "think which reaction comes first – the 'oooh' or the 'ahhh'? When 'oooh' comes first and 'ahhh' follows, you have done the right thing. But if the 'ahhh' precedes the 'oooh,' you have probably made the wrong decision."

–Heard from Rabbi Yisroel Gordon

"Today everyone wants instant gratification no matter how long it takes."

"Experience is the hardest teacher. It gives you the test first, and the lesson afterward."

Integrity

An impoverished widow once came to the courthouse of the great sage, Rabbi Yehoshua Kutner. Weeping bitterly, she begged the Sage to summon a man she claimed had wronged her.

Rabbi Yehoshua ordered the accused individual to appear before the court, but adamantly refused to preside over the case himself. Instead, he referred the case to another rabbi.

"The Torah forbids the taking of bribes," Rabbi Yehoshua explained. "Do you think that a bribe is only a gift of money? Tears can also be a bribe that 'blinds the clear-sighted' – especially the tears of a poor widow."

–*Maayanah Shel Torah*

"Rationalize = Rational lies."

"It's easy to be pleasant when everything goes like a song, but the worthy man can smile when everything goes dead wrong."

"Self-control is knowing you can but deciding you won't."

Intention

One afternoon, a king was feeling weary and decided to take a short nap. He ordered his private servant to instruct the members of the palace to keep quiet in order to allow his Majesty to sleep.

Obediently, the servant began walking around the palace, hushing the members of the palace with a "shaa" sound. The others, intrigued by his strange actions, began to imitate him, assuming that the king had asked everyone to behave in this manner. One by one, everyone began saying "shaa," until they recited the chant in unison.

As this mania spread through the palace, the outside guards followed suit. The onlookers and tourists beyond the palace gates witnessed this new procedure and assumed that this was the conduct expected as they neared the king's palace. Eventually, this practice spread until the entire city was reciting "shaa," in subservience to the king, imagining that this was the king's desire.

An hour later, the king emerged from his quarters and summoned his private servant. When the servant appeared, the king admonished him, exclaiming, "Although your intentions were proper, I have not been able to rest!"

—Diary of a Chassid,
from the Rebbe's farbrengen, Shabbos Beraishis 5717

Interdependence

After purchasing a ticket for a peaceful ocean cruise, the passenger hopped onto the boat to enjoy the ride. In the middle of the trip, he felt extremely thirsty. He resolved to casually drill a hole beneath his seat and drink from the water that would seep through the bottom of the boat.

"Hey, Sir! What do you think you are doing?" shouted the captain when he noticed the man's drilling.

"I'm just making a small hole under my seat," the passenger replied innocently.

"Don't you know that you're not allowed to do that?" the captain demanded.

"Why?" the man retorted. "It's my seat – I paid for it! And besides, I'm not harming anyone else!"

"Leave everything a little bit better than how you found it."

"Beware of small expenses; small leaks sink ships."

Internalization

One bitterly cold night, Reb Shmuel Munkes embarked on a journey to his Rebbe, Rabbi Schneur Zalman of Liadi. The wind pierced his bones, and he was relieved to see a wagon passing by. The wagon stopped, and the driver happily offered Reb Shmuel a ride. The driver was a liquor merchant, and Reb Shmuel made himself comfortable among the many bottles of liquor that filled the wagon. Still chilled to the core, Reb Shmuel realized that drinking some of the vodka would warm him. The driver agreed, and after drinking the vodka, Reb Shmuel felt warm through and through.

Reb Shmuel entered into a private audience and told Rabbi Schneur Zalman, "The Rebbe has taught his chassidim that they must take lessons from every life experience." Reb Shmuel recounted the events of his journey. "The air had chilled me to the bone. I sat among the bottles of liquor for quite a while, and although liquor has the power to warm a person, I still remained ice-cold. Only when I actually drank the vodka did I become warm."

Reb Shmuel said that this taught him an important lesson about Divine service. One might dwell in an environment of Torah, surrounded by inspiration, yet only once it is internalized will it have a great affect on him and warm his soul.

*"Education is what remains with you
after you've forgotten all that you learned."*

Investment

Meir's rash had become unbearable. Over a month had passed, and the red, itchy blotches were becoming redder and itchier! Exasperated from the discomfort and worried that he may have a serious condition, he decided to make an appointment with the doctor.

After his examination, the doctor prescribed an ointment and predicted that the rash would disappear within three days.

"That's it?" exclaimed Meir, wondering how such a persistent ailment could be cured so quickly.

"No," replied the doctor, "that's after four years of medical school, and ten years of practice!"

—Heard from Yossi Mizrachi

Comment:

Often, an action or experience that appears insignificant may be valuable. Our actions should be estimated by the past effort that brought us to this point. Only after many years of toil in medical school could the doctor prescribe the ointment.

Similarly, the *Amida* prayers are built upon the merit of all the preceding prayers. One "little" *mitzva* we perform adds to the good deeds accumulated by our ancestors, and can "tip the scales" to bring *Moshiach*.

Judgment

Once, during a private audience, the Rebbe quoted a passage from the *Talmud* that states, "Even the wicked are full of *mitzvos* like seeds in a pomegranate."

This Talmudic statement had bothered the man visiting the Rebbe for some time. He challenged the Rebbe, "If they are wicked, how can they possess so many *mitzvos*?"

The Rebbe smiled and explained his own question on the statement: "If they possess so many *mitzvos*, how can they be considered wicked?"

–Heard from Rabbi Akiva Wagner

"Everything is relative."
—Albert Einstein

"In judging yourself use your mind, in judging others, use your heart."

"Don't judge those who try and fail. Judge only those who fail to try."

"The difference between a flower and a weed is judgment."

Light

Once a wise king wished to marry off his favorite daughter. He devised a contest to establish which eligible bachelor would qualify for this tremendous privilege. The king announced that anyone who wanted to marry the princess must report to the palace and fill up a room with a light substance, in a short amount of time.

The first brave contestant approached the palace with garbage bags full of feathers. He strove valiantly to fill the large room with feathers, but time ran short and he failed.

The next day, another suitor attempted to quickly fill the room – this time with delicate silk. Time ran out again, and he too left the palace disappointed.

The contest continued day after day, as hundreds of contestants hoped to pass the test and win the king's daughter, but no one succeeded. The king began to despair. Wasn't anyone in the kingdom qualified to marry the beautiful princess?

One day, a young man arrived at the palace empty-handed. The king wondered how this boy planned to win the contest.

Entering the room, the young contestant put out the lights. He reached into his pocket, retrieved a small candle and lit it. The light spread throughout the entire room, illuminating the darkness. The king rejoiced at finding the perfect match for his precious daughter.

–Heard from Rabbi Tzemach Cunin

Comment:

The Rebbe has revealed the secrets to bring *Moshiach*. One of the Rebbe's campaigns is that every Jewish woman and girl, from the age of three, should light a *Shabbos* candle with a blessing. This small light spreads throughout the world, shedding spiritual light on our generation and dispelling the forces of darkness.

"All the darkness in the world
cannot even extinguish a small candle."

"A Mitzva, like a pebble tossed in a pond, ripples on and on."

Love

A fisherman once caught a salmon. When he saw its extraordinary size, he exclaimed, "This is wonderful! I'll take it to the Baron, because he loves salmon."

The poor fish consoled itself; "There's hope for me yet."

The fisherman brought the fish to the manor house, and the guard at the entrance asked, "What do you have?"

"A salmon," answered the proud fisherman.

"Great," said the guard. "The Baron loves salmon!"

The fish felt that there was some corroboration of the facts. The fisherman entered the palace, and though the fish could hardly breathe, it still had hope: The Baron loves salmon.

The fish was brought into the kitchen, and all the cooks commented how much the Baron loves salmon. The fish was placed on the table, and when the Baron entered, he ordered, "Cut off the tail, cut off the head, and slit open the salmon!"

With his last breath, the fish cried out in despair, "Why did you lie? If you really love me, care for me and let me live. You don't love salmon, you love yourself!"

–Adapted from "Simple Words"

Luck Vs. Logic

Luck and Logic once went hiking on a road. At dusk, Luck turned to Logic and exclaimed, "After so many hours of hiking, I'm exhausted. It's time to rest!" He pitched his tent and made himself comfortable where he stopped, right in the middle of the road.

"Are you crazy?" Logic asked Luck. "On the road? Use your logic for a moment and pitch your tent on the roadside!"

"Absolutely not!" Luck insisted. "This is my luck; here I stopped, here I stay."

Logic, of course, set up his tent on the side of the road.

In the middle of the night, a large eighteen-wheeler truck zoomed down the road. The road was dark, and it was difficult for the driver to see. When the truck neared Luck's tent, it was too late to stop. To avoid disaster, the driver swerved to the side of the road, missing Luck's tent by merely an inch, crashing into Logic's tent...

–Heard from Yosef Konikov

Comment:

We plan and G-d decides. We must make plans – but remember Who ultimately has the last decision.

Masks

Chassidim in Lubavitch would customarily wear long jackets. One chassid, however, wore a short jacket when he was in Moscow on business, and changed into a long jacket when he returned home to Lubavitch.

Once, before entering into a private audience with the Rebbe, Rabbi Shmuel of Lubavitch, the chassid deliberated: 'Why should I wear my long jacket for my private audience with the Rebbe? The Rebbe knows who I am. Why try to fool him? I will be myself!'

Thus, the chassid entered the Rebbe's study wearing a short jacket.

"Why are you wearing a short jacket?" the Rebbe asked.

The chassid was shocked. He explained honestly, "Rebbe, I did not want to fool you!"

"Fool me?" the Rebbe asked. "Until now I thought you were a chassid trying to fool the business world. Now I see you are a businessman trying to fool the chassidim."

–Heard from Rabbi Shloima Zarchi

Comment:

Sooner or later a man who wears two masks forgets which one is real.

"Rather than 'Fake it till you make it',
you should 'Be real till you feel real.'"
—Chana Burston

Merchandise

A G-d-fearing Jew once embarked on a long overseas journey. He was one of many traveling with valuable merchandise, planning to spend several months overseas selling their goods, and hoping to return with a significant profit.

One evening, far out at sea, the merchants saw a threatening storm in the distance. Everyone panicked, but the Jew escaped to a corner and prayed to G-d that they should reach shore safely.

The ship began swerving from side to side; huge waves of water splashed in, and the boat began to sink. The captain announced that to lighten the boat, everything heavy must be cast into the sea. The merchants watched aghast as the crew cast the expensive merchandise overboard.

The ship eventually docked safely. Although the merchants were thankful to be alive, they were upset at losing their money and belongings. Only one person showed no sign of sadness – and that was, of course – our dear Jew.

It was not long before the Jew was asked by one of the other merchants, "Sir, aren't you upset at losing all you owned? Why do you look happy?"

"I still own my possessions," the Jew answered, "I never lost them."

The merchant was astonished. The Jew explained, "You see, the merchandise I had aboard was not significant to me, for I did not consider it my life. My life is Torah and its commandments and my connection to G-d, and that I have not lost!"

–Mishlei Chachomim, Chumash Beis Yehuda

"There must be more to life than having everything."

"Money may be the husk of many things, but not the kernel.
It brings food, but not appetite;
medicine, but not health;
acquaintances, but not friends;
joy, but not happiness.
It is good to have money and the things that money will buy.
It is also good to make certain that we have not lost
the things that money will not buy."

"The real measure of a man's worth is
how much he would be worth if he lost all his money."

"Money can't love you back."
—Bank ad

"People make money – not the other way around."

Mission

One *Shabbos*, Shmerel was called to the platform of the synagogue to perform *hagba*, the lifting of the Torah scroll. It was a heavy Torah scroll; yet Shmerel thought he would be able to do it, as he was a husky fellow. But Shmerel overestimated his strength, and, to his embarrassment, almost dropped the Torah scroll! He even required assistance returning the Torah scroll to its place.

Shmerel resolved not to return to the synagogue without doing a full workout, which would surely prevent such an embarrassment from recurring!

Three months later, a well-built muscle-man entered the synagogue. He looked quite different, but yes – it was Shmerel. When Shmerel heard his name called, he strode to the platform, confident that this time he would not fail. Shmerel raised the Torah scroll aloft, and didn't even have to bend his knees. The "oohs and ahhs" from the congregants brought a satisfied smile to Shmerel's face, and he sat down with the Torah scroll, waiting for someone to wrap it in its mantle.

Suddenly, the *gabbai* approached him and said, "Shmerel, you did a remarkable job! But we called you up for an *aliya*, not for *hagba*!"

–Heard from Rabbi Dovid Hazdan

Comment:

A job can be done remarkably, but was it the job that was demanded?

91

Modification

Once, in a very small town, in a very small synagogue, a very big problem arose! A new Torah scroll cover was donated to the synagogue. All the congregants struggled with all their might to fit the Torah scroll inside its new cover. No matter how strong or clever the congregants were, they could not fit the scroll inside. The frustration in the very small synagogue quickly spread to each very small home in the very small town. No one could think of a solution, so they called upon their very wise sage.

He stroked his beard and said, "If the cover doesn't fit on the Torah scroll, we must cut down the Torah scroll so that it fits the cover."

The townspeople celebrated thinking their problem had been solved.

Comment:

Ridiculous? Of course! The cover must be altered. This theme is similar to the saying of the post-war Chassidic leaders, "We will not modify the Torah to fit America. We will tailor America to fit the Torah."

"Without tradition new things die."

Nature Vs. Nurture

A host and his guest were discussing philosophies of education. One advocated not giving children any religious instruction, calling it "conditioning." The host did not respond, but invited his visitor to the garden.

Upon entering the garden, the visitor was surprised to see nothing but huge tangles of weeds.

"Why, this is not a garden," he exclaimed. "There is nothing but weeds here!"

"Well, you must understand," answered the host, "I do not wish to infringe upon the liberty of my garden in any way. I allow it to express itself freely and produce whatever it thinks is best."

"If you think education is expensive, try ignorance."

"To decide not to decide is a decision."

"Great men are not born, they develop. Only infants are born."

*"Vacant lots and vacant minds
become dumping grounds for rubbish."*

Optimism

The Rebbe suffered a serious heart attack in 1977. The following day, the Rebbe insisted on delivering a discourse, as he had done on that same day for the previous thirty-eight years.

A few days later, the doctor asked, "How is the Rebbe feeling?"

"Physically, thank G-d, I feel fine," the Rebbe replied, "but mentally, not so well." This, the Rebbe explained, was because he had not visited and prayed at the gravesite of his father-in-law, as he was accustomed to doing several times a month.

"You must take care of your health," the doctor insisted. "If not, there is a twenty-five percent chance of a relapse." The doctor asked the Rebbe if he understood his warning.

"Oh, yes," answered the Rebbe with a smile. "You said that even if I don't take care of my health – which, I assure you, I will – there is a seventy-five percent chance that there won't be a relapse."

–Souvenir Journal, Kislev 5758, South Africa

"Think positive and the result will be positive:
An optimistic thought has the strength
to rescind a heavenly decree."
—Adapted from the Rebbe

"A pessimist sees the difficulty in every opportunity;
an optimist sees the opportunity in every difficulty."

Overkill

Reminiscing about his 1992 visit to Israel, Zelig recalls an experience in a Jerusalem frozen yogurt shop:

"This was a unique treat for me, because at that time it wasn't easy to buy kosher frozen yogurt in New York.

"First you could choose between a chocolate or vanilla base. Then you could add the flavors of your choice, all featured in the display. The variety ranged from fresh strawberries and peaches, to crunchy wafers and nuts. Not knowing when I would be offered this luxury again, I decided to indulge...

"'I'll have strawberries,' I told the cashier excitedly, 'and pineapple; wafers, and white chocolate, and some of this too...' I ordered anything I thought would make the yogurt taste even more delicious.

"The cashier may not have cared, or she thought I was a spoiled American. In any case, she obediently fulfilled my requests.

"But I was disappointed. It did not taste like any of the flavors I had chosen... None of them were distinct..."

Comment:

Too much of something, even something good, may not be good. It's all about balance.

For example, there are two ways to design a beautiful bouquet of flowers: You can combine a variety of brightly-colored flowers, but the effect may be "too much;" none of the colors will be distinct. Or, you can select several specific colors, and each color will shine for its true worth.

Rabbi Levi Wineberg, head of the Lubavitcher Yeshiva in South Africa, puts it quite well: "If you see someone with more than two or three books open in front of him, he probably isn't learning anything."

"Experience is what you get
when you don't get what you want."
—Old Yiddish saying

Perfection

The students of the Maggid of Mezritch were immersed in discussing the profound mystical concepts that their Rebbe had taught that morning. Amongst them sat Rabbi Schneur Zalman of Liadi.

One student raised a thought-provoking question. "How would you create the world if you were G-d?"

The students contemplated quietly and prepared their answers.

"If I were G-d, I would have changed this and this!" responded the first.

"But if I were G-d, I would have changed that and that!" answered another.

Each student pointed out faults in the world, arguing that they should be eliminated.

When Rabbi Schneur Zalman was asked for a response, he innocently replied, "If I were G-d, I would have created the world just as it is!"

"No one is 100% perfect –
but there is someone 100% perfect for you."
—Rabbi Chaim Binyomin Burston

Perspective

Standing by his wagon, the wagon driver donned *tallis* and *tefillin* and recited the morning prayers. In the midst of his prayers, he realized that his wagon was broken. He became occupied with fixing his wagon and was distracted from his prayers.

Rabbi Levi Yitzchak of Berditchev, who is legendary for judging favorably, noticed this scene. He raised his hands toward heaven and proclaimed, "G-d Almighty – see how wonderful Your children are. Even while working, they pray to You!"

–Heard from Zevi Raskin

"Success and failure does not depend on circumstance,
but on your approach to the circumstance."
—Rabbi Dovid Hazdan

"We all live under the same sky,
but we don't all have the same horizon."

"We all look at the same world;
but what we see depends on who we are."
—Rabbi Isaac of Homil

Planning

The famous Torah scholar, Rabbi Yonason Eibshitz, was an advisor for the king.

Once, while strolling down the streets of Vienna, the king met his wise advisor and friend. After greeting each other amiably, the king asked his Jewish subject where he was going.

"I don't know," Reb Yonason replied in all honesty.

The king's eyes flashed with sudden anger. Friend or not, how dare he trifle with his Majesty! The king ordered his guards to have the advisor arrested and imprisoned. However, before the day was over, the king relented. "After all," the king thought to himself, "this is my wise advisor; he couldn't have meant to slight me. There must be an explanation for his behavior."

The ruler visited the eminent scholar in his cell. "Look here," he scolded, "how dare you trifle with your King so frivolously?"

"I didn't mean to trifle with you, your Majesty," explained the scholar ruefully. "You did not ask me where I was *planning* to go; you asked me where I was *going*. I really did not know where I was going. It must be clear to you by now. You see, earlier today I had planned to go study and pray at the synagogue, and instead I ended up in jail!"

"We plan and G-d laughs; Plan all you want – it's healthy – but remember Who ultimately has the last laugh."

Practice

His dream was finally fulfilled. After many years of suffering behind the Iron Curtain, Meir was allowed to travel to the Holy Land.

It was what he had always envisioned, "a land flowing with milk and honey." Feeling elated, Meir walked from field to field. He soon encountered an exquisite orchard, rich with luscious fruit, and he happily sat on a bench to relax beneath a large shady tree. "An ideal place for a snack!" Meir thought. He picked a fruit, made a blessing with great enthusiasm, and enjoyed every bite.

As he ate, the outraged owner of the orchard sat on the bench beside him. "My dear friend," said the owner with disdain, "don't you know that it says in the Torah: 'Thou shalt not steal?'"

Meir leaned back on the bench, took a deep breath, put his arm around the owner, and said, "Wow! Israel is truly amazing: Crisp air, beautiful scenery and delicious fruit. And, to top it all off, while enjoying all these pleasures, someone comes and shares a word of Torah!"

"He who learns and learns, but acts not upon what he knows, is like one who plows and plows, but never sows."

"In theory, there is no difference between theory and practice. But, in practice, there is."

Prayer

Every night, Zissel served her husband Mendel the same awful dinner: Burnt chicken and burnt potatoes. One evening, Zissel stayed in the kitchen for hours cooking. Mendel could hear his wife working with vigor. Pots and pans clicked and clanged harmoniously. Imagining the delicacies that Zissel must be preparing, Mendel's mouth watered. "She is taking so long..." he mumbled. "Finally I will eat a gourmet dinner!"

Triumphantly, Zissel emerged from the kitchen. She placed a plate before her famished husband, and to his horror, it was the same burnt chicken and burnt potatoes that she served every night!

—Heard from Rochel Holtzkenner

Comment:

Every morning, G-d waits for us to pray, but we often don't perform this service with proper intention. If we delay our prayers, they must reflect proper preparation, and should not merely be the same "burnt chicken" we've been saying daily.

Preaching

"You know, you always manage to tell people a *'gut vort'* (a thought provoking teaching)," commented a young man to a renowned lecturer. "And you always add that the purpose of hearing a *vort* is that it not remain a *'gut vort.'* Rather, the inspiring thought should be internalized and practiced, resulting in a 'good deed.' Yet you yourself never practice what you preach?!"

The lecturer reflected for a moment, stroking his long white beard, and replied, "Hmmm... That's a *'gut vort!'*"

"After all is said and done,
much more is said than done."

"Many things are true in spirit,
but the ultimate test of truth is here on earth."

"Well done is better than well said."

"If you must speak your mind,
then mind how you speak."

"Most of us would get along well
if we used the advice we give others."

"He is a wise man who knows what not to say."

"A wise man thinks what he says; a fool says what he thinks."

Precedence

Plush white carpets lay upon the floor of the newly renovated home.

The mother of the family distributed a small jar of honey to each of her children in honor of the festival of *Rosh Hashanah*. As she handed the honey to her eager children, she blessed them that their coming year should be as sweet as the honey.

A little while later, the youngest child ran to her mother, sobbing and choking on her tears. After calming the child with that special 'mother's touch,' she asked her daughter what had happened. The child bashfully admitted, "My jar of honey fell and cracked, and the honey leaked onto the brand new white carpet!"

The mother patted her child lovingly and replied, "That's alright, sweetheart. I'll buy you another jar of honey."

"I've learned to pick my battles;
I ask myself, 'Will this matter one year from now?
How about one month? One week? One day?'"

"Sometimes, 30% off means paying 70%
for something you really don't need."
—Bank ad

Prevention

"Should I go to college and become a doctor, or to *yeshiva* and become a Rabbi?" a young student asked the Rebbe in a private audience, commenting that he gravitates to the former.

"To *yeshiva* and become a rabbi," the Rebbe replied. Then the Rebbe added, "A doctor cures someone who is *already* ill. A rabbi prevents people from *becoming* ill."

Comment:

We often inordinately emphasize the effect rather than the cause. For instance, if a rotten apple is causing a disturbing odor, rather than spraying air-freshener, get rid of the apple!

*"People who don't learn from history
are destined to repeat it."*

*"Date yourself first. Then ask yourself:
Would you want to date yourself again?"*

*"Each problem solved
becomes a rule that solves other problems."*

*"Don't tell G-d how big your problems are.
Tell your problems how big G-d is."*

Priorities

Rabbi DovBer of Lubavitch, son and successor of Rabbi Schneur Zalman of Liadi, was known for his unusual powers of concentration. While engaged in study or prayer, he did not hear or see anything around him.

Once, while deeply immersed in study, Rabbi DovBer's baby, who had been sleeping in a nearby cradle, fell out and began to cry. Rabbi DovBer was so immersed that he did not hear the baby's cries and continued studying.

The infant's grandfather, Rabbi Schneur Zalman, was on an upper floor of the house and was also studying, yet he heard the baby's cries. He interrupted his studies, went downstairs, soothed the infant, and returned it to its cradle. Rabbi DovBer still did not notice.

Later, Rabbi Schneur Zalman reprimanded his son, "No matter how lofty a Jew's pursuits, he must always hear the cry of a child."

This story was told not only to those who must take care of children: parents, teachers and other adults, but also to children, for this story has an important lesson for children as well.

Everyone has a "Good Inclination," rooted in the Divine soul, that plants good thoughts into a Jew's head, and an "Evil Inclination," rooted in the animal soul, that plants bad thoughts into his head. The Evil Inclination is the "older" one, for it comes early in the life of every child to tempt him to do things he shouldn't. The Good Inclination is the "baby."

Sometimes, just when a child should do something important, such as studying, homework, and the like, he desires to do something else, which may be good in its proper time, but is not appropriate now.

For example, when it is time to do homework, the child wants to put his room in order, or run an errand. Worse still, the Evil Inclination tempts him to do something he should never do. The Good Inclination "baby" then feels cast out of its cradle, unhappy, and begins to cry.

This story reminds us to hear the cry of the "baby" – the Good Inclination – and bring it fulfillment by doing the right thing at the right time, and not the wrong thing at any time.

–Based on a letter of the Rebbe, dated 17 Shvat, 5723

Protection

1974: Arab terrorists invade the Holy Land, murdering and destroying property. At Ma'alot School, a busload of children from nearby Tzefat are brutally murdered. The world is shocked. The Rebbe calls for a strengthening of spiritual defenses, emphasizing the *mitzva* of *mezuza*.

At one of many public addresses on the subject, the Rebbe related: "I received a call from Tzefat. The caller checked the *mezuzos* at the yeshiva where the children had been studying and seventeen *mezuzos* were found non-kosher. Seventeen children from that *yeshiva* were killed.

"G-d forbid to say," the Rebbe continued, "that it was the absence of kosher *mezuzos* that caused these children's deaths. Heaven forbid! However, just as a soldier must wear a heavy helmet to protect himself from enemy bullets, likewise, the *mezuza* protects the Jew. The helmet may be heavy and costly, and it may even disturb one's concentration.

"If he does not wear the helmet and is hit by enemy fire, it is the enemy who killed him, not the lack of the helmet. Yet wearing the helmet would have saved him..."

–Mezuza Campaign Flyer, Chabad House, Johannesburg

"Better have it and not need it, than need it and not have it."

Psychosomatic

The businessman had spent a hard day at work, and had been looking forward to dining at a restaurant as relaxation. A waiter approached him, and while unbuttoning his top button and loosening his tie, the man ordered his favorite dish. "If at all possible," he added, "please lower the heating." The waiter nodded in agreement, and went to the back room.

Upon returning with the order, the waiter noticed that the man sat bundled in his coat. Responding to the waiter's expression of surprise, the man explained that it had become far too cold! The waiter again headed for the back room.

A short while later, the diner rang his bell to catch the waiter's attention. The waiter responded politely and offered his services. "Sorry for bothering you again, Sir, but now it is far too hot!" With seemingly boundless patience, the waiter smiled in sympathy and headed yet again to the back room.

An old lady, sitting at the last table at the back of the hall, had witnessed the entire scene. She looked in astonishment at the waiter and remarked, "Isn't he driving you crazy?"

The waiter winked. "The joke is on him. I'm not doing anything in the back room!"

Purpose

Once a king had a faithful water-carrier. Every morning the water-carrier went down to the river with two buckets strapped to a rod upon his shoulders. He would fill each bucket with clean, cool water, and set out along the path to the king's palace.

As he walked down the path, the water in one of the buckets would drip out slowly. This bucket was old and worn, and had small holes in its bottom due to many years of usage. By the time the water carrier reached the palace, the bucket would be empty. The other bucket, however, was almost new and always managed to bring the king a full bucket of water.

After many days, the old bucket felt frustrated.

"I am useless!" the old bucket complained. "You fill me up with clear, fresh water for the king, but by the time we arrive at the palace, it has all leaked out! Why don't you throw me away?"

"Dear bucket," the water carrier said gently, "you are not useless. Tomorrow I will show you your purpose."

The next morning, the water carrier trudged down to the river and filled up his two buckets. They began walking along the path toward the palace. "Look below you," the water carrier told the old, broken bucket. "What do you see?" Beneath him the bucket saw a trail of exquisite flowers resting among luscious, green grass.

The water carrier switched his buckets. The old bucket was now in the hand with which the water carrier usually held the strong bucket.

"Now what do you see beneath you?" he asked the old bucket. The bucket saw that the path beneath him was made of scorched, dry dirt.

"You see," the water carrier explained to his old bucket, "every day, I sprinkle little seeds along the path. With your help, I water them as we walk to the palace. Afterward I cut the lovely flowers and put them on the king's table to beautify his throne. You are very special."

Comment:

We often experience difficulties, and feel "worn out" when we do not achieve what we had hoped to. Even if we think we've failed, our bucket seems empty by the time we reach the king, we should know that every experience plants seeds within us. When tended carefully, these seeds can grow into beautiful gardens and make us stronger, more developed people.

"Know that the true worth of your travels lies not in your destination, but in who you come to be along the way."

"When you win, nothing hurts."

Quality

"Is anyone here wearing a Borsalino brand hat?" a respected rabbi asked his *yeshiva* students.

Many of the students were wearing such a hat, yet they sat sheepishly. None of them was brave enough to respond. They assumed that their rabbi would ridicule them for caring about something so materialistic.

Finally, one student bashfully raised his hand.

The rabbi turned to him and said, "Ahh! Now I have someone to talk to. Someone who appreciates class and beauty in life! With a person like this I can speak about the beauty and true quality of Judaism."

"Once, special people were famous.
Nowadays, famous people are special."

"It's not the hours you put in your work that counts,
it's the work you put in the hours."
—Sign hanging in Cheder Menachem Office

"What counts is not how old you are, but how you are old."

Recognition

As a child visited the bank for the first time, he watched the teller dispense thousands of dollars to one customer and collect thousands of dollars from another. The child marveled at the amount of money being handled before his eyes. As he left, the child turned to his father and said, "That man behind the counter must be a millionaire; did you see all the money he had?"

"Not so," the father said. "You and I may be wealthier than he. The money he takes and dispenses is not his, but the bank's. If he abuses this privilege and gives away or keeps one extra dollar, he can lose his job and the privilege of handling any money at all. He must always bear in mind the money's origin and to whom it belongs."

–Adapted from "The Maggid Speaks"

Comment:

Our talents and wealth we accumulate is ours only because G-d has given them to us to serve Him.

We are G-d's bankers.

"Every day is a gift. That's why we call today 'the present.'"

"Some people make a big fuss over a comet in the sky, but never notice a sunset."

Reflection

A mother led her young son to the bottom of a deep valley, and said, "Scream the words, 'I hate you' as loud as you can."

He yelled at the top of his lungs, "I HATE YOU!" Suddenly, he heard the overwhelming sound of, "I HATE YOU, I Hate You, I hate you!" echoing around him.

She turned to her son and requested, "Now, scream the words, 'I love you' as loud as you can."

He yelled at the top of his lungs, "I LOVE YOU!" Suddenly, he heard "I LOVE YOU, I Love You, I love you!" echoing around him.

"Gaze into a lake and behold a mirror of water reflecting your image. Love another soul and his love will mirror back to you."
—Adapted from the Tanya, Chapter 46

Relaxing

Levi was a hard-working counselor at a Jewish summer camp. One afternoon he was sitting at the flagpole seemingly doing nothing. Pesach, the learning director, while making his rounds during classes, observed Levi in this idle state, and asked, "Levi, why aren't you doing anything?"

Levi, looking at his intruder as if Levi was, in fact, presently engaged in an activity, replied, "Pesach, I am doing something!"

"You cannot appreciate a day off school,
if you don't go to school;
you cannot enjoy a day off work,
if you don't go to work."

Reputation

One *Yom Kippur,* as the Maggid of Dubno entered the synagogue, he noticed that it was more crowded than usual. People he had never seen were attending the service. He ascended the pulpit and addressed the congregation with the following parable:

A merchant once toiled for many years and established a prosperous business. However, due to a series of poor investments, he eventually lost all his wealth, and was even in debt to one creditor for 8,000 rubles.

The poor merchant felt miserable. To whom could he turn? His friends advised him to approach his creditor and plead his cause.

When the creditor heard the man's woeful tale, he said sympathetically, "Stop crying! You owe me nothing. I'm ripping up your promissory notes and starting a clean slate. May you succeed at restarting your business. You can count on me for help!"

When another businessman heard of this creditor's fabulous generosity, he tried his luck at liquidating his debt with the same creditor. He assumed he would surely succeed, as he owed 5,000 rubles less than the other merchant! That evening he approached the creditor and related his feigned sob-story.

"Stop crying," cautioned the creditor. "It will do you no good. You must pay every cent of the 5,000 rubles you owe me."

"But why did you forgive the other merchant?" he demanded.

"How can you compare yourself to him?" asked the creditor. "I have been doing business with him for years. He has proven his trustworthiness. And you? I hardly ever see you! You seem to visit me only when I offer bargains."

The Maggid of Dubno concluded his speech and gazed seriously at his large audience. "Need I be more explicit?" he asked as he left the pulpit.

–Heard from Yossi Greenberg

*"Don't be afraid of going slowly;
be afraid of standing still."*

Retrospect

"How can G-d allow tragedies to happen?" an Israeli army general once complained to his rabbi. In anguish, he added, "I have lost a young child and best friend."

"Picture this scene," the rabbi began. "Thousands of armed soldiers stand together. Someone approaches one of the soldiers and asks, 'What are these implements you are wearing?' The soldier responds that these are weapons used to kill people. Some of the ammunition can even kill thousands of people at once.

"The man screams in fear, 'Save me from these murderers!' The soldier calms him, explaining, 'The only way you can live peacefully in the city is through the protection of armed soldiers.' The man relaxes and thanks the soldiers profusely.

"What has transpired here?" asked the rabbi. "One moment the man is screaming in fear, and the next moment he is filled with gratitude. What caused this drastic change?

"Only the man's knowledge has changed," The rabbi explains. "Until then, he had not known who the soldiers were and what they represented. After learning of their noble purpose, his attitude changed completely.

"The same applies to us," the rabbi concluded. "Our problem is that we do not see G-d's perspective. If we would, we would realize that everything He does is for the good."

Sacrifice

As a young Lubavitch *yeshiva* student, Rabbi Yosef Wineberg was once challenged about outreach.

Another Orthodox Jew argued, "Although spreading Judaism is important, outside influence is harmful to the children whose families are involved in outreach. Instead of teaching estranged Jews, we should devote our energy to strengthening our own children."

"Imagine a house burning down," the man continued. "Only select furniture can be rescued. Some furniture is half-burnt or almost ruined, and some is untouched. Would you bother to salvage the furniture that had been seriously damaged? Just preserve the fresh furniture!

"Similarly," he explained, "we should only devote ourselves to the education of our own children..."

Rabbi Wineberg thought for a moment and responded, "That applies to saving furniture in a burning house. But what if *people* are trapped? The healthy ones can liberate themselves with minimum assistance. But those who are burnt and suffering need someone to carry them out of the fire and heal them..."

–Heard from Rabbi Levi Wineberg

Comment:

Our responsibility to educate other Jews does not detract from our responsibility to educate our own children. On the contrary, both paths of education must merge and complement each other.

*"Nowadays we must live with self-sacrifice,
not die with self-sacrifice."*
—Rabbi Adin Steinsalz, in "The Long Shorter Way"

*"A flame can give of its fire again and again
and not be diminished. Be a flame."*

*"Every time you give up something you crave
for something worthwhile, you become stronger."*

Self-Refinement

"A Jew is like a candle," the Rebbe once explained to a chassid, "and his task is to light up other Jews."

The chassid asked, "Rebbe, did you light my candle yet?"

The Rebbe replied, "No, but I have given you the match. You must now strike it and ignite yourself."

"If you want to fix the world, start with yourself."

*"Be so busy improving yourself
that no time is left to criticize others."*

"He who rows the boat doesn't have time to rock it."

*"Before we awake, the neshama of the day calls out
and pleads, 'Please make the most of me!
I will only exist once.
The sun will rise and set – and I will be gone.
Make me purposeful and accomplish
all that you are meant to in me.'"*
—Adapted from the Zohar

*"When the day comes that I must account for my life, I will not
be asked: 'Why weren't you Moses?' I was not equipped to be
Moses. But I dread the question, 'Why weren't you Zusia?'"*
—Reb Zusia of Anipoli

Sensitivity

An illiterate farmer hired a scholarly young man to reside in his ranch and educate his children.

One day, a telegram arrived for the farmer, but due to his ignorance, he asked the scholar to read it to him. The scholar opened the letter, read it quietly, and then read it aloud:

"The telegram reads: 'Son, your father has passed away. Please make every effort to attend the funeral.'"

Before the scholar had finished reading, the farmer gasped and fainted.

After reviving him, the scholar turned to the farmer and asked, "I don't understand. I read the letter first, so why didn't I faint as well?"

The farmer, still in shock, snapped back angrily, "Because it's not your father!"

"Disagree without being disagreeable."

Superiority

As a small child, Reb Zalman Aharon (the "Raza"), the older brother of Rebbe Sholom DovBer of Lubavitch (the "Rashab"), often complained that he was noticeably shorter than his younger brother.

One day, the Raza sneaked up behind his brother and pushed him lightly into a small ditch. As the Rashab stood up in surprise, the Raza seized the moment and pointed out that now he was taller.

Rabbi Shmuel of Lubavitch, the father of the two boys, observed the entire episode. The Rebbe asked for a chair, ordered the Raza to stand on it, and asked him, "Tell me, who's taller now?"

The Raza answered excitedly that yet again he was taller.

"Aha!" said Rabbi Shmuel. "There you are! To be bigger than your friend, there is no need to pull him down. Simply elevate yourself!"

"An argument is an exchange of ignorance.
A conversation is an exchange of intelligence."

Temptation

An addicted smoker visited a therapist to help him quit. The doctor admitted, "I too used to smoke. I tried quitting by convincing myself that cigarettes are disgusting, harmful to my health, dangerous to my family, and detrimental for my position in society.

"After this inner tirade, I would quit. But several days later I would wake up again and forget my decision completely. 'Maybe smoking is not so terrible?' I would rationalize. 'And what if I don't smoke around my family, but where nobody sees?'

"This pattern repeated itself constantly. My rationalization brought me to relapse.

"Once," the therapist explained excitedly, "I tried a different strategy. I took a cigarette in my hand, looked at it and told myself, 'Yes, this cigarette will bring me pleasure. I want to smoke it. But I will quit!'"

"This approach worked, and I have not smoked a cigarette since. The reason this technique succeeded is that I didn't fool myself by trying to feel repulsed by cigarettes. Instead, I admitted to myself that I desired it, yet chose to control my desires."

"Do not say 'I am nauseated by pork' or 'I do not want to wear clothes made of a mixture of wool and linen' but say, 'I want to eat pork and wear forbidden mixtures, but what can I do? My Father in Heaven has decreed that I may not.'"
—Toras Kohanim, 9:10. Quoted in Rashi, Leviticus, 20:6

Thankfulness

An Israeli couple eulogized their only son emotionally. The audience in the synagogue listened with sympathy as the couple spoke of the young boy's special character, appreciation for life, and deep devotion to the Holy Land of Israel. Just after his nineteenth birthday, he was brutally killed while defending his beloved Land. In their son's memory, the parents presented a generous donation to their synagogue.

After the presentation a woman in the audience turned to her husband and whispered, "Let's donate the same for our son."

"What are you talking about?" asked the father. "Our boy didn't lose his life."

"That's just my point," replied the mother. "Let's give charity because he was spared."

Toil

A bird lay in the desert dying of thirst. Its weak body was showing indications that the end was near, so it whispered to G-d, "Please give me water and spare my life."

Suddenly, a fierce wind erupted and lifted the bird, sending it sailing through the air until it was just a few feet from the riverbank. "Please, G-d," the bird whispered. "I'm so tired and thirsty. I can't walk all the way to the river!"

Again the wind lifted the bird until it was just one foot away from the cool water. "Oh, please G-d! It's too far for me to walk! I'm so thirsty. Please give me water to drink!"

Yet again the wind carried the bird until it lay at the riverbank. "G-d, I'm so thirsty. Please save me!" it desperately cried. A final gust of wind lifted the bird, placing it right inside the cool, fresh water. Despite its amazement, the bird foolishly continued praying for the water that its body so desperately required.

A heavenly voice called out and admonished it, exclaiming, "Silly bird! See that I have carried you to the water. You need only bend your head and drink! This only you can do."

*"Even if you're on the right track,
you'll get run over if you just sit there."*

"Genius is 1% inspiration and 99% perspiration."

Torah

During the era of Roman domination over the Land of Israel, religious expression and study of Torah were forbidden. Offenders were punished with cruel tortures, and even with death.

The Jewish leaders risked their lives to teach Torah and encouraged the Jewish people's adherence to its laws.

Once, Papus ben Yehudah saw Rabbi Akiva publicly teaching Torah. He asked him, "Do you not fear punishment by law?" Rabbi Akiva answered with a parable:

> A fox, strolling along the riverbank, notices fish swimming around. He asks, "Why are you running?"
>
> "We are afraid of the net that people set up to catch us," they reply.
>
> The fox persuasively reasons, "Perhaps it would be wise to ascend to the shore and live with me, as my parents lived with your parents."
>
> The fish wisely reply, "You speak foolishly; if we are afraid in our natural habitat, our fear will be even greater on land, where death will be certain."

Rabbi Akiva concluded: "The Jew, as the fish in the water, must be immersed in his soul's nourishment – the Torah and its commandments. If now, as we sit and engage in Torah, about which it is written 'For it is your life and the length of your days,' we are in such danger, without it, we will surely perish."

When Papus was also arrested, and placed in the same prison as Rabbi Akiva, he told Rabbi Akiva: "Fortunate are you, Rabbi Akiva, that you were arrested on account of words of Torah; woe to Papus who was arrested on account of idle things."

—Talmud, Berachot 61b

"There are many roads, all leading to the same destination."

*"It's not hard to make decisions
when you know what your values are."*

"Acting good is a giant step closer to being good."

"Make a good habit and it will make you."

*"We are what we do repeatedly.
Excellence, then, is not an act, but a habit."*
—Aristotle

*"Acting good can make you good.
Acting happy can make you happy."*

Transformation

Once there was a powerful king, who ruled many lands. His most precious treasure was a diamond – the most flawless diamond in the world. Once, at a royal party, the king flaunted his diamond, passing it from guest to guest as it rested on a soft velvet pillow. Abruptly, the diamond fell and became deeply scratched.

The ruler summoned his diamond experts to correct the blemish. However, the distraught king learned that they could not remove the blemish without cutting the surface, thus reducing the diamond's value.

Finally, a craftsman appeared and assured the king that he could fix the diamond without reducing its value. The self-confidence this artist displayed convinced the king to entrust the diamond's repair to him.

Several days later, the artist returned with the diamond. The king was astonished to see that the ugly scratch had disappeared. In its place a beautiful rose was engraved.

The scratch had become the stem of an exquisite flower.

"Failure is success… if we learn from it."

Transitions

The auspicious day of *Yom Kippur* was imminent. Before *Yom Kippur* it is traditional for men to immerse themselves in the *mikva* several times.

One fellow, obviously unaccustomed to going to the *mikva* with others around, drew attention to himself. As he prepared to enter the water, the other men saw that he was trying to conceal something on his arm. Just before he reached the water, he slipped and lost his balance. Trying to catch his fall, he let his hand off his arm, revealing a lewd tattoo.

Completely ashamed, he stood frozen in his spot. Everyone was at a loss for words to comfort him until an old man said, "Look here, my boy, I also have a tattoo." He pointed to the row of numbers etched in his skin. "This is in case I forget what those monsters had planned for me... It seems we've *both* come a long way."

Comment:

It's not where we are coming from, but where we are going that matters. Furthermore, all Jews can connect with one another, despite outward differences. In essence, all Jews are one, and by searching, we can reveal this inner bond.

"'Teshuva' is returning to our source.
We may cross a bridge and feel accomplished,
yet realize that a new, higher bridge lies ahead.
Once that is successfully crossed,
an even higher bridge awaits..."

Trust

The summer sun shone mercilessly. Acres of freshly grown crops began to dehydrate, and flocks of animals searched in vain to quench their thirst.

In desperation, a group of farmers gathered in the synagogue to pray for rain.

After listening to the passionate prayers, a little boy asked his father if the men truly expected rain. "Of course," replied his father. "Otherwise, we wouldn't be here."

"But father," the child protested, "why hasn't anyone brought an umbrella?"

Use

Once there was an adolescent camel that would pose questions to its mother incessantly, as all children naturally do.

"Mother, why do we have a hump perched on our backs?"

Mother replied, "My child, these humps prevent hunger and thirst as we trek through on long journeys through the dry desert. We store rations of water inside our humps to quench our thirst."

"But mother, why do we have long eye-lashes?"

"Oh, son, those are to keep the sand in the desert from ruining our eyes during sandstorms. This protection allows us to continue traveling."

"And what about our awkwardly-shaped feet?"

"Aha! They support our legs from sinking into the soft sand. This enables us to walk more easily and quickly."

Finally, frustrated and confused, the young camel cried out, "So what are we doing in the Bronx Zoo?!"

Value

Once, while a king was hunting in the forest, night fell earlier than expected. The king and his entourage could not find the path back to the palace. After hours of wandering, they glimpsed a light glowing in the distance. Feeling optimistic, they headed toward it.

The flickering light illuminated a small cottage, which was occupied by an old man. The host warmly invited his guests to stay for the night, and diligently cared for their needs. Before leaving, the king invited the old man to the palace to repay him for his kindness.

When the appointed time arrived, the king offered the old man his most precious singing bird, one that the king so delighted at listening to that he placed it adjacent to his bed. Although the king regretted losing the bird, he was pleased to reciprocate the good deed.

On another trip to the forest, the king surprised the old man with a visit. In the midst of conversation, the king inquired after the extraordinary bird.

"Oh, the bird?" asked the old man. "It was scrumptious. As soon as I got home, I treated myself…"

Viewpoint

Although the elderly man had not driven in many months, he finally mustered the courage. As he cautiously cruised down the side roads, his tension subsided. He merged onto the highway, trying to allow his automatic "driving nature" to rule his maneuvering.

As he increased speed, his cell phone rang. It was his wife.

"Listen, dear," his wife said nervously, "The radio announcer says that there is a madman driving on the wrong side of the highway, against the traffic. Please be careful!"

"Only one mad driver?" he yelled. "They're *all* driving the wrong way!"

"Never be afraid to stand with the minority when you feel the minority is right, for one day the minority that is right will be the majority. Always be afraid to stand with the majority that is wrong, for one day the majority that is wrong will be the minority."

"Normal is boring."
—Chaim Bryski

"Code of Jewish Law rules that one ascertains whether a duck is kosher if it swims against the tide. That's the powerful challenge of living in our times – to fight ferocious tides..."
—Chana Burston

Warmth

One winter day, a man discovered a thick layer of frost on his window. He started painstakingly scraping it off.

"What are you doing?" inquired a curious neighbor.

"Removing the frost from my window," answered the man, "so I can see outside."

His friend saw that the labor was tedious and advised him, "Light a fire in your home – the frost will disappear by itself!"

"Put on a coat and you will be warm.
Light a fire and you will warm up others."

Welcoming G-d

"Young man," the Rebbe of Pscizcha demanded, "Where can one find G-d?"

"Everywhere," answered his disciple, who was to become the Rebbe of Kotzk. "His glory fills the universe."

"Young man," the Pscizcher repeated. "I asked you, where could one find G-d?"

The Kotzker was quiet. "Well, if I don't know, then please tell me," he requested.

The Pscizcher then said, "Listen, young man. G-d can only be found where you let Him in."

–Heard from a great-grandson of the Rebbe of Kotzk

Comment:

While traveling on the subway, an acquaintance of ours would announce, "G-d is homeless. Is anyone willing to take Him in?"

"It is there inside. Everything is there inside.
But the 'I' stands firmly at the gate."
— From "Bringing Heaven Down to Earth"

"Make yourself small and you will be greater.
Know you're nothing and you will be infinite.
At the very least, don't make a big deal of yourself
and you will be all that much closer to the truth."

Worth

A man risked his life by swimming through the treacherous riptide to save a youngster being swept out to sea. After the child recovered from the harrowing experience, he thanked the man for saving his life.

The man looked into the boy's eyes. "That's okay, kid. Just make sure your life was worth saving."

—From "Shabbat Talk," South Africa

"You don't choose how you're going to die or when, but only how you are going to live."

"The value of life lies not in the length of days, but in the use we make of them; a man may live long yet live very little."

*"Do more than exist - Live.
Do more than look - Observe.
Do more than read - Absorb.
Do more than listen - Understand.
Do more than think - Ponder.
Do more than talk - Say something."*

"More important than adding years to your life, is adding life to your years."

"The tragedy of life is what dies inside a man while he lives."
—Albert Einstein

"Just one more spoonful, please?"

Instant Chicken Soup

A Russian Jewish immigrant entered an American supermarket for the first time. He looked around in amazement, as if he were in the middle of an incredible museum.

As he browsed through the aisles, he encountered an item called "instant coffee." His American friend explained that by pouring the powder into hot water, delicious coffee could be created instantly! This amazed the immigrant. Next he discovered milk powder, "kool aid" powder, and even mashed potato powder. He was fascinated. Finally he noticed "baby powder," but this he could not fathom.

He turned to his friend and cried, "No way! Impossible! It takes time and effort to turn a person into a *mensch!*"

—*Heard from Rabbi Yossi Goldman*

Comment:

Perhaps the same applies to "instant chicken soup."

Once, when something was ailing us, and our bodies needed to be warmed, we would run to our mothers' or grandmothers' home for freshly cooked chicken soup. This "Jewish penicillin" never failed. It was the real thing, rich with flavor, labor and love.

Similarly, when we needed to warm our *neshamos*, we would go to our Rebbe, teachers, *mashpi'im*, and parents. They would share a "spoonful" of a Torah thought – sometimes packaged in a story. The story was not an end in itself, but a means to grasp and internalize the rich Torah thought behind it.

Today, the seekers of instant gratification avoid the labor of that traditional "Chicken Soup," and have invented "instant chicken soup."

However, for the traditionally potent "Chicken Soup" that was passed from mother to daughter, and teacher to student, that heals, warms and inspires us internally, we need the authentic, full-flavor, full-effort chicken soup. The instant one just isn't the same.

Each story and insight shared within this book can be viewed as a spoonful of that rich "Chicken Soup." Instead of being regarded as an "instant" story with a punch line, each story and saying must inspire our lives with its message.

"Words that emanate from the heart penetrate the heart."
—Sefer Hayashar

"Why did G-d create us with two ears but one mouth?
To teach us to listen twice as much as we speak."
—Rabbi Moshe Herson

"Thought is the blossom, language the bud,
and action the fruit behind it."

Insights

Chicken Soup and the Neshama

An advertisement for a restaurant in upstate New York reads:

"Eat here or we both starve."

This is a great motto for the *neshama*'s descent to this world. Had the *neshama* remained in the Garden of Eden, it would have enjoyed a life of spiritual bliss. But G-d wants us to make a spiritual life in this world; to transform the physical into spiritual.

Chassidus teaches we are not to seclude ourselves and be "spiritual" by neglecting our bodies. By working with our bodies, they will act as a vehicle to elevate the *neshama*.

Otherwise, both the body and soul will starve.

Life

We can ride a ferry across the river with two attitudes, reflecting two approaches to life.

One attitude is to impatiently await arrival at the other side. We are so concerned with our destination that we are oblivious to our surroundings.

Or we can enjoy the scenery and our fellow passengers.

Either way, we reach the other side of the river. But in the second case our trip is more enjoyable.

Clothed Minded?

Clothes, the ones that make their way into your closet as impulse buys, gifts or obligatory purchases for compulsory events, are about ourselves. What we actually decide to put on our backs each day and venture into the world in has nothing to do with trends or marketing. It has to do with whom we want to show the world we are. Or who we want to convince ourselves we could be.

So perhaps people aren't the slaves to trends that the fashion industry has so long depicted them as being; perhaps trends are a slave to the individual, who uses them to say something about him/herself...

Clothes are really identifiers of each person as a performer in his own life...

One reason that clothing can stereotype us so inescapably is that even the most minute detail can signify an entire personality type...

The clothes we choose are a better indicator of who we think we are than our faces or our bodies, which we did not choose... They can be a mirror of what's inside, or a map to display our aspirations.

We are what we wear...

–Excerpts from an article in the New York Times Magazine, Nov. 14 1999

"The mask, given time, comes to be the face itself."

"It's all in the presentation."

Today

There are two days in every week that we should not worry about - two days that should be kept from fear and apprehension.

One of these days is "Yesterday," with its mistakes and cares, its aches and pains, its faults and blunders. Yesterday is beyond our control. No amount of money can recover it. Yesterday is gone.

The other day we should not worry about is "Tomorrow" with its burdens, adversities, and great promise. Tomorrow is also beyond our control. Tomorrow's sun will rise either in splendor or behind a mask of doubts - but it will rise. Until then, we have no stake in tomorrow, for it is unborn.

This leaves only one day - "Today." With G-d's help, we can fight the battles of Today.

It is only when we insist on carrying the burdens of those two awful eternities - Yesterday and Tomorrow - that we break down. It is not challenging experiences that harm us, but bitterness and paralysis from Yesterday, and anxiety and dread of Tomorrow.

Let us journey together one day at a time.

–Adapted from "School Update" Torah Academy of South Africa

"The past has gone;
the future is yet to happen;
the present disappears with the blink of an eye.
So why worry?"
—Ibn Ezra

No Deposit, No Return

A valuable lesson can be learned from the soda bottle:

"No Deposit, No Return."

We'll only gain from life as much as we're willing to invest.

Limitations

Why did the journey from Egypt to the Holy Land take the Jews forty years?

Taking the people out of Egypt took a moment, but taking Egypt out of the people took forty years...

Equality

Why do chassidim dance in a circle?

In a circle no one leads or follows. Everyone is equal.

Redemption

One of the major holidays in the Chassidic calendar is the 12-13th of Tammuz, which is called, "the holiday of redemption." On this day Rabbi Yosef Yitzchak, the Previous Lubavitcher Rebbe, was released from imprisonment for the "sin" of spreading Judaism in Soviet Russia.

The Previous Rebbe writes in his memoirs that he was informed that he would be set free on the 12th of Tammuz. However, the offices were closed due to a local holiday, and the Rebbe was not released until the 13th of Tammuz.

If so, why do we celebrate the Chassidic holiday also on the 12th of Tammuz? True, the 12th of Tammuz was the Previous Rebbe's birthday, but both the 12th and the 13th are known as "the holiday of redemption." On the 12th of Tammuz the Rebbe was still in prison. Shouldn't the "holiday of redemption" be commemorated only on the 13th?

Perhaps the reason is that, though the Rebbe was in prison on the 12th of Tammuz, he was in a "state" of redemption; he was to leave the following day. Indeed, the same dark prison walls surrounded him, but the atmosphere was redemptive.

Exile is likened to prison. The Rebbe has promised us that we will soon be released. This message imbues us with the strength to overcome the painful and difficult tests of exile. The dark world is the same, yet the Rebbe instills within us an atmosphere of redemption.

May we experience the actual redemption speedily in our days with the coming of Moshiach.

Do You Know Your Bride?

Why does the groom place an opaque veil over his bride's face?

The father of the first Jewish family, Jacob, was a victim of a last-minute switch. His father-in-law substituted Leah, the older of his two daughters, for Rachel, the one whom Jacob loved. Jacob discovered the deception only after he had consummated the marriage with Leah. Jacob, choosing to accept his fate, remained with Leah, and later also married Rachel, the bride of his choice.

Why did the first Jewish family have to emerge in such an enigmatic manner?

Leah represents fate – she is the woman who Jacob ended up marrying. Rachel represents choice – she is the woman who Jacob chose to marry. When you get married, although you may think you are marrying Rachel, there is bound to be some element of surprise, and you will discover that you also ended up with Leah, who represents those elements of your spouse you never knew you were getting. These elements, however, may be exactly what you need.

---

*) Insights from pages 146-154 were written by Rabbi Yosef Y. Jacobson.

When the groom veils his bride, he is saying, "I will love, cherish and respect not only the 'you,' which is revealed to me, but also those elements of your personality that are hidden from me. As I am bonding with you in marriage, I am committed to creating a space within me for the totality of your being – for all of you, all of the time."

Under the Veil

Our Sages say that "Abraham our father instituted the morning prayers (*Shacharis*), Isaac the afternoon prayers (*Mincha*) and Jacob the evening prayer (*Maariv*)."

The Chassidic Masters offer the following homoletical interpretation: Jacob instituted the prayer for the bride under the veil. Just as the evening service occurs when night falls and one's sight is eclipsed, so too the bride's prayer under the veil is eclipsed. However, unlike the evening service that has words, the bride's prayer is a prayer that has never been put into words, for it transcends the human vocabulary.

The Circle

A Jewish wedding consists of three circles: the feminine circle, the masculine circle and the Divine circle. The *chupa* ceremony begins with the bride encircling the groom. She walks around her husband-to-be seven times; the groom then encircles her finger with a circle-ring. All of this occurs under a canopy, which represents G-d's encircling embrace of the couple.

A circle, which has no beginning and no end, represents infinity. It is only through marriage that the bride and the groom become infinite, as they are empowered to become G-d-like and create life.

Silence

Under the *chupa* the groom says to the bride: "You are hereby consecrated to me with this ring, in accordance with the law of Moses and Israel." The bride remains silent. She does not even verbally acknowledge her groom's words and gift.

For if the bride were to speak during these moments, she would reveal the deepest secrets of the soul, and the world is not yet ready to hear them.

When *Moshiach* comes – when the world will have reached its spiritual zenith – the bride will speak under the *chupa* canopy. As the prophet Jeremiah says, "There will be heard in the cities of Judah and in the streets of Jerusalem, the sound of joy and the sound of gladness, the sound of the groom and *the sound of the bride*" (Jeremiah 33, 10-11).

Mistakes in Life

When the groom breaks the glass under the *Chupa*, everyone shouts: "*Mazal Tov!*"

When your husband 'breaks something' during your life together; when your wife 'breaks something' in the years to follow, what should you do? You too should shout, "*Mazal Tov!*" and give thanks.

Say, "Thank you G-d for giving me a real person in my life, not an angel: A mortal human being who is characterized by fluctuating moods, inconsistencies and flaws."

Who's Coming?

The holy Reb Yisroel of Ruzhin said: "Not only is it announced in heaven whom you will marry, they also announce the location, the date and the people who will attend the wedding."

Selflessness

The holy Rebbe of Socotshav said: "It is only through marriage, when man sheds his individualistic character for the sake of his wife, that a Jew can begin experiencing himself as part of the collective Jewish people."

Do the Dishes

A man once came to the Rebbe, lamenting the fact that his relationship with his wife was on the down side.

"I heard," said the man to the Rebbe, "that folding one's prayer shawl on Saturday night, after *Shabbos*, is propitious for bringing peace and harmony to the Jewish home. Should I begin following that custom?" asked the man.

"That might be a good idea," responded the Rebbe, "but I have a better idea: wash the dishes after *Shabbos*."

Men are from Za,
Women are from Malchus

In the *Kabbala*, man is compared to a soul, women to a body.

The source of the body is infinitely deeper then the source of the soul. The soul originates in G-d's projective self; the body stems from G-d's intimate self.

That is why the elements of Jewish observance that were granted to men are projective oriented, for the most part, whereas the elements of Jewish observance granted to the female are of an intimate and subtle nature.

Paradoxically, it is only the soul that brings to the fore the tremendous depth embedded in the body.

In *Kabbala*, the story of man and women is put thus: Men are from *Za*, G-d's projective attributes; women are from *Malchus*, G-d's inner dignity.

"Mine Says"

Once, as Rabbi Schneur Zalman of Liadi, stepped out of his room, he overheard his wife remarking to several women, "Mine says..."

The Rebbe responded, "With one commandment I am yours, with how many are we G-d's!" whereupon he fell onto the doorpost in deep transcendental meditation.

Upon awakening he said, "Go out and see daughters of Zion" (Song of Songs 3:11). Stepping out of one's self and perceiving the Divine Truth, comes from the daughters of Zion, *Malchus* arousing *Za.* In the future, "A women of valor shall be the crown of her husband."

"What" and "Who"

Feminine energy is who you are; masculine energy is what you do. Man conquers; woman reveals. Man is aggressive; woman is subtle. Man gives love; woman is love.

That is the reason that the status of a Kohanite, Levite or Israelite is established through the father, and the status of a human being as Jew or non-Jew follows the matriarchal lineage:

A Kohanite, Levite and Israelite vary in their occupational work. A Jew and non-Jew vary in their essence.

From your father you learn the things you must do. From your mother you learn who you are.

A Soul

The body readily submits to the guidance and inspiration of its soul, because it knows that it is in good hands.

A woman will readily commit herself with joy and gladness to her husband, if he behaves like a soul, not like a beast.

Who is the Boss?

A man once came to the Rebbe lamenting the fact that his wife did not listen to him. "A wife is supposed to obey her husband," said the man to the Rebbe.

"Of course," said the Rebbe, "I agree. But why, indeed, should a woman listen to her husband?"

"What do you mean?" replied the frustrated husband, "because the man is the master of his home."

"Wrong," said the Rebbe with a smile, "because the man ought to behave in such a noble way that his wife gladly wishes to do things for him."

The Miracle of Marriage

Marriage is the most supra-rational and supra-natural event in life.

The basic rule in existence is that one and one makes two.

Marriage is a declaration, that one and one makes one.

That is why it is so important to have G-d as a third partner in your marriage, so that He will perpetuate that miracle every moment of your life.

A Taste of Infinity

In many Jewish communities, a man begins donning a prayer shawl during prayers only after he enters into marriage.

There are two types of garments: One type is a garment that is measured to fit the body of the wearer, such as a suit, a shirt, a coat, and so forth. The other type of garment is not measured because it does not need to have a specific size, like a prayer shawl, which envelopes the entire body – an infinite attire, an unlimited garment.

It is the woman who grants her husband the taste of infinity.

One, Two, Three

Marriage comes in three forms: The singular marriage, the twosome marriage and the three-dimensional marriage.

In the singular marriage, one individual is dominated and consumed by the other party. The ego of one swallows up the partner's existence.

In the twosome marriage, each partner preserves his/her distinctions, making their marriage an exercise in argumentation, divisiveness and strife.

Then there is marriage in its true sense – the three-dimensional marriage, where two individual people join to create a third reality – a life together.

That is why the Torah was given in the third month of the Jewish calendar, the month of Sivan: The purpose of Torah is to create a three-dimensional marriage between G-d and his world.

Vulnerability

The role of a husband is to subdue his ego to his wife, and thus create an atmosphere where the women's energy can emerge.

The role of a wife is to give her husband a sense of safety and confidence to subdue his ego and celebrate his vulnerability.

Intimacy

Why is intimacy so awesomely powerful?

Because it is the only experience in life that allows us to become truly G-dlike, in that it gives the husband and wife the power to create.

Nothing else we do as human beings is as G-dlike as creating a new life, which in turn can create more life, on and on into eternity.

This G-dly nature is what gives sexuality its mystique. It is the one opportunity man has to 'taste' G-d – to think as He thinks and to create as He creates.

King and Queen

"A groom is likened to a king; a bride to a queen. How long does this continue?" a groom asked his rabbi.

"As long as you treat your wife as a queen, you are a king," the rabbi responded.

Defining Love

"Love," the Rebbe explained to me, "is not as portrayed in romance novels. It isn't an overwhelming, blinding emotion."

"These books do not portray real life," the Rebbe said. "It is a fantasy, a make-believe world with made-up emotions. Fiction is just that – fiction. Real life is different."

I had been discussing with the Rebbe some suggested matches, and explained why none of them appealed to me.

Then, as father to daughter, he explained the meaning of real love.

"Love," he told me, "is an emotion that increases in strength throughout life. It is sharing and caring, and respecting one another. It is building a life together, a unit of family and home.

"The love that you feel as a young bride," he continued, "is only the beginning of real love. It is through the small, everyday acts of living together that love grows and flourishes.

"The love you feel after five or ten years is a gradual strengthening of bonds. As two lives unite to form one, with time, one reaches a point where neither partner can visualize life without their mate by their side."

Smiling, the Rebbe told me to put the romantic notions developed by my literary involvement aside, and view love and marriage in a meaningful way.

I walked out of the Rebbe's office with a huge smile. The Rebbe knew how to communicate with a dreamy young girl. He knew what to say and how to say it. His words, spoken from the heart, reverberated within my heart.

–Excerpts of an article by Chana Sharfstein

*"It is more important to go together
than to know where you are going."*

*"If you are close when you should be far,
you will be far when you should be close."*
—The Rebbe

*"Men may be from Mars and woman from Venus;
the challenge is to make it work on Earth."*

*"Love does not consist of gazing at each other,
but of looking in the same direction."*

Got Ingredients?

Too many cooks can't spoil the broth.

Perhaps you have stories, insights or sayings that yield a powerful lesson.

Readers like you submitted many of the stories in this book. We invite you to share some "soup" for our next publication. It could be a story, parable, insight, saying or even a cartoon. Submissions may be original or something you heard or read. Share it with us, so we can share it with others.

Stories should be short, and have life-long lessons.

We also welcome your comments and suggestions.

Please send submissions to:

Chicken Soup to Warm the Neshama
c/o Pesach & Chana Burston
submissions@ChickenSoupNeshama.com

Both you and the author will be credited for your submission.

Glossary

770 – 770 Eastern Parkway, Brooklyn, New York; the address of Lubavitch World Headquarters

Akiva, Rabbi – leading Mishnaic authority; martyred by the Romans circa 138

Aliya – (lit. ascent) term used referring to calling someone to the Torah reading in the synagogue

Amalek – a Biblical Canaanite nation descending from Esau and a legendary foe of the Jewish people

Amida – (lit. standing) also referred to as *Shemona Esrei* (*Eighteen Benedictions*); the main section of all obligatory prayers, recited standing

Bachya ibn Paquda, Rabbi – 1040-1080; eleventh century sage and writer on Jewish thought; his most acclaimed work is *Chovas Halevavos* (*Duties of the Heart*)

Bar Mitzva – (lit. son of the command) a Jewish boy who reaches the age of thirteen, the age of adulthood in Jewish life, thus becoming religiously responsible for his own conduct; also refers to the event marking this milestone

Chabad – (a) acronym for *Chochma, Bina* and *Daas,* meaning "wisdom, intellect and understanding," denoting the three intellectual faculties spoken of in Jewish mystical thought; (b) the Chassidic movement, synonymous with Lubavitch and founded by Rabbi Schneur Zalman of Liadi, which focuses on incorporating G-dliness into our lives through intellectual study of G-d (utilizing the *Chabad* faculties to govern the *midos*), joy, love of G-d, and love of fellow man

Chassid – (pl. chassidim) (a) one who goes beyond the letter of the law (b) an adherent and follower of a Chassidic Rebbe

Chassidism – the practices and beliefs of the Chassidic movement, emphasizing attachment to G-d, love of G-d, joy in Divine worship and brotherly love

Chassidus – Chassidic thought

Chupa – wedding canopy

DovBer of Mezritch, Rabbi – ?-1772; second leader of the Chassidic movement

Elimelech of Lisensk, Rabbi – 1717-1787; Chassidic Rebbe, brother of Rabbi Zusia from Anipoli

Farbrengen – Chassidic gathering

Gabbai – the person responsible for the proper functioning of a synagogue or communal body

G-d – in Jewish belief, any word that is used as an appellation of G-d must be treated respectfully; it is common to avoid spelling out the entire word in case the paper upon which it is written be discarded in an undignified manner

Gimmel Tammuz – Hebrew date of the passing of the Lubavitcher Rebbe, Rabbi Menachem M. Schneerson, on June 12, 1994

Hagba – the ritual of lifting the Torah and displaying it to the congregation after the Torah reading

Hashem – G-d

Hayom Yom – (lit. *From Day to Day*) an anthology of aphorisms and customs, arranged according to the days of the year, assembled from the talks and letters of Rabbi Yosef Yitzchak of Lubavitch (1880-1950), sixth Lubavitch Rebbe; compiled by Rabbi Menachem Mendel Schneerson, seventh Lubavitch Rebbe

Hiskashrus – the bond between a chassid and a Rebbe

Isaac of Homil, Rabbi – one of the leading chassidim of the first three Chabad-Lubavitch Rebbes; head of the Rabbinic Court in Homil

Israelite – member of the Jewish people, not descending from the tribe of Levi

Kabbala – (lit. received tradition) the mystical tradition that is an integral part of Judaism

Kohanite – priest, descending from Aaron the High Priest

L'chaim – (lit. to life) traditional words of toast offered on alcoholic drinks

Levi Yitzchok of Berditchev, Rabbi – 1740-1809, Chassidic leader known for his compassion for and defense of the Jewish people

Levite – descendant of the tribe of Levi

Lubavitch – (Russian: town of love), (a) town in the county of Mohilev, White Russia, which served as the center of the *Chabad* Chassidic movement for four generations; (b) the *Chabad* Chassidic movement, which became known as the Lubavitch movement

Maggid – preacher

Maggid of Dubno – Rabbi Yaakov Kranz, 1741-1804; famous European preacher, best known for his parables

Maggid of Mezritch – see DovBer of Mezritch, Rabbi

Maimonides – Rabbi Moses ben (son of) Maimon, known by the acronym of his name the "RaMBaM," 1135-1204; one of the foremost Jewish thinkers of the Middle Ages; his *Mishna Torah* is one of the pillars of Jewish law, and his *Guide to the Perplexed* – a classic in Jewish philosophy.

Malchus – (lit. sovereignty) the last of the ten *sefiros* (Divine attributes spoken of in Jewish mystical thought), embodying G-d's royalty, speech, feminine aspect and power of creation

Mashpia – (lit. source of flow) in Chassidic circles, a spiritual mentor

Mazal Tov – (lit. good luck) Congratulations!

Meir of Premishlan, Rabbi – Rebbe in Premishlan

Mendel Futerfas, Rabbi – 1906-1995; a renowned *mashpia* of the twentieth century and *Chassid* of *the* Rebbe

Mendel of Kotzk, Rabbi – 1787-1859; a Chassidic Rebbe, forbearer of the Gur dynasty

Mensch – Yiddish: a person of integrity and honor

Mezuza – (pl. *mezuzos*; lit. doorpost) a small parchment scroll affixed to a doorpost, which contains two Torah portions (for protection)

Midrash – the classical collection of the Sages' homiletical teachings on the Torah

Mikva – body of water for ritual immersion effecting purification (from ritual or spiritual defilement or unsuitability) and/or spiritual elevation

Minyan – quorum of ten males over the age of thirteen, necessary for communal prayer services

Mitzva – (pl. *mitzvos*; lit. commandment) one of the Torah's 613 Divine commandments; a good deed or religious precept

Moshiach – (lit. the anointed one) the Messiah

Neshama – soul

Rashab – see Shalom DovBer of Lubavitch, Rabbi

Rashi – Rabbi Shlomo Yitzchaki; 1040-1105; fundamental commentator on the *Tanach* (bible) and Talmud

Rav Huna – Talmudic sage

Reb Zusia – see Zusia of Anipoli, Rabbi

Rebbe – (lit. my teacher) Chassidic Master

Rebbe, The – Rabbi Menachem M. Schneerson, 1902-1994; seventh Rebbe of Chabad-Lubavitch, building upon and expanding his predecessors' work to revolutionize Jewish life across the globe; known throughout the world simply as "the Rebbe"

Rosh Hashana – (lit. head of the year) the Jewish New Year Holiday celebrated on the Hebrew date of 1-2 Tishrei

Schneur Zalman of Liadi, Rabbi – 1745-1812; author of the *Tanya* and *Shulchan Aruch*; founder of the Chabad (Lubavitch) Chassidic movement and its first Rebbe

Shabbos – the Sabbath

Shalom DovBer of Lubavitch, Rabbi – 1860-1920; Fifth Chabad-Lubavitch Rebbe

Shliach – emissary; commonly denoting the emissaries of the Rebbe

Shlichus – the act of going out on a mission, often referring to the Rebbe sending out *Shluchim*

Shmuel Munkes, Rabbi – one of the leading Chassidim of Rabbi Schneur Zalman of Liadi; known for his wit and "Chassidic pranks"

Shmuel of Lubavitch, Rabbi – 1834-1882; fourth Chabad-Lubavitch Rebbe

Tallis – prayer shawl fringed at four corners, worn by men during certain prayer services

Talmud – the basic compendium of the Oral Law, comprised of the *Mishnah* and its two commentaries, The *Jerusalem Talmud* and the *Babylonian Talmud*

Tammuz – the fourth month of the Jewish year (when counting from *Nissan*)

Tanya – basic work of *Chabad* Chassidism written by its founder Rabbi Schneur Zalman of Liadi

Tefillin – phylacteries; black leather boxes, containing Torah portions written on scrolls, wrapped on the arm and head of adult men during weekday morning prayers

Teshuva – (lit. return) returning to G-d; in the narrower sense, the act of repentance from sin

Torah – (lit. teaching) (a) The Five Books of Moses (The Bible); (b) the Divine teachings of G-d encompassing the whole body of Jewish law, practice and tradition

Tzefat – Safed

Vort (Gut Vort) – (Yiddish, lit. (good) word) a thought provoking teaching or remark

Yeshiva – academy of Torah learning

Yisroel Baal Shem Tov, Rabbi – 1698-1760; founder of the Chassidic movement

Yisroel of Ruzhin, Rabbi – 1797 - 1851, Chassidic Rebbe

Yochanan HaSandler, Rabbi – second century Talmudic Sage

Yom Kippur – Day of Atonement, Jewish Holiday observed on the tenth day of the Hebrew month of Tishrei

Yonasan Eibshitz, Rabbi – Talmudic Scholar and Rabbi of Homburg and Prague in the era of Rabbi Yisroel Baal Shem Tov

Yosef Yitzchak of Lubavitch, Rabbi – 1880-1950; Lubavitch, Warsaw and New York; sixth Rebbe of Chabad-Lubavitch

Yud – the tenth letter of the Hebrew alphabet

Yud Tes Kislev – (lit. the nineteenth of Kislev), anniversary of the passing of the Maggid of Mezritch in 1772; anniversary of the release from capital sentence and prison of his disciple, Rabbi Schneur Zalman of Liadi, in 1798

Z"A – acronym for *Ze'er Anpin* (lit. small face) denoting the first six *midos* (of the ten *sefiros* spoken of in Jewish mystical thought)

Zohar – basic work of *Kabbala*; compiled by 2nd century mishnaic sage Rabbi Shimon bar Yochai

Zusia of Anipoli, Rabbi – 1718?-1800; disciple of Rabbi DovBer of Mezritch; famed for his simple ways and self-effacement

Permissions

Grateful acknowledgment is made to the following for permission to reprint previously published material:

(Dis)Ability. Reprinted by permission of ArtScroll-Mesorah Publishers, from "Echoes of the Maggid" by Rabbi Pesach Krohn. © 1999 Mesorah Publications, Ltd.

Balance. Reprinted by permission of Rabbi Tzvi Freeman, from "Bringing Heaven Down to Earth." As well as a quote from "Be Within, Stay Above." © 1996, 1997, 2000 Rabbi Tzvi Freeman. *www.theRebbe.com*

Fear. Reprinted by permission of Rabbi Simon Jacobson from "Toward a Meaningful Life." © 1995 William Morrow and Company, Inc. *www.meaningfulife.com*

Incentive. Reprinted by permission of Chabad.org, from "Chabad Online Weekly Magazine" Behar-Bechukotai 5761, adapted from Shmuos V'sipurim from Rabbi Z.S. Dvorkin by Yanki Tauber. *www.chabad.org*

Love. Reprinted by permission of Simon and Schuster Adult Publishing Group, from "Simple Words: Thinking About What Really Matters in Life" by Rabbi Adin Steinsaltz. © 1999 Adin Steinsaltz.

Recognition. Reprinted by permission of ArtScroll-Mesorah Publishers, from "The Maggid Speaks" by Rabbi Pesach Krohn. © 1987 Mesorah Publications, Ltd.

Insights p.146-154. Reprinted by permission of Rabbi Yosef Y. Jacobson. © 1999 Yosef Y. Jacobson. *YYJacobson@aol.com*

Stories and Sayings to submit for further editions:

submissions@ChickenSoupNeshama.com

About the Authors

Pesach and Chana Burston founded Chabad of Orange County, New York in 2004 and presently reside with their four children in Monroe, NY.

As executive directors, they promote and teach Torah and Judaism by providing enrichment and education to the many they reach through creative programing, classes, and, of course, stories.

They can be reached at 845-782-2770, rabbi@ChabadOrange.com, chana@ChabadOrange.com or visit www.ChabadOrange.com